# Barbara Brackman's
# Civil War Sampler

## 50 Quilt Blocks with Stories from History

C&T PUBLISHING

Text copyright © 2012 by Barbara Brackman

Photography and Artwork copyright © 2012 by C&T Publishing, Inc.

Publisher: Amy Marson

Creative Director: Gailen Runge

Art Director: Kristy Zacharias

Editor: Deb Rowden

Technical Editors: Sandy Peterson and Helen Frost

Cover/Book Designer: April Mostek

Production Coordinator: Jenny Davis

Production Editor: S. Michele Fry and Joanna Burgarino

Illustrator: Tim Manibusan

Photography by Christina Carty-Francis and Diane Pedersen of C&T Publishing, Inc., unless otherwise noted

Published by C&T Publishing, Inc., P.O. Box 1456, Lafayette, CA 94549

Library of Congress Cataloging-in-Publication Data

Brackman, Barbara.

Barbara Brackman's Civil War sampler : 50 quilt blocks with stories from history.

    pages cm

Includes index.

ISBN 978-1-60705-566-2 (soft cover)

1. Patchwork--Patterns. 2. Quilting--Patterns. 3. United States--History--Civil War, 1861-1865. I. Title.

TT835.B6364 2012

746.46--dc23

                          2012019273

Printed in China

10 9 8 7 6 5 4 3

*Sesquicentennial Sampler,* 48″ × 48″, by Barbara Brackman, Lawrence, Kansas; machine quilted by Lori Kukuk, 2011

I stitched 12″ × 12″ blocks, using patterns drafted especially for this book. I chose the bright palette typical of appliqué quilts during the Civil War years, one not often used for reproduction samplers. With 3″-wide finished strips and 3″ × 3″ cornerstones, nine blocks make a cheerful baby quilt.

# Contents

**On the cover:** Detail of *Liberty & Union*, shown in full on the title page, 89½″ × 105″, by Becky Brown, Montpelier, Virginia; machine quilted by Deb Jacobs, 2011

I sent the patterns to Becky before making the blog postings and she made the 8″ × 8″ blocks ahead of time to give blog readers fabric and color ideas. She'd just retired and was looking for a challenge. Before long, she was the volunteer pattern tester. Her end-of-the-year comment:

*"There is no way I could have known what I was getting into with joining an online quilting project! I can't really think of the right words, if there are any, to tell you all how special this year [was] because of this quilt project and the many wonderful quilters I now call friends."*

She used 50 blocks, set on point in a lovely sashing pieced of three strips, each finishing to 1″ (cut 1½″ × 8½″). The cornerstones are 3″ × 3″ finished nine-patches stitched from squares (cut 1½″ × 1½″). The inner border finishes to 2½″ wide and the outer border to 5½″ wide. Note: Several of the quilts shown in this book are made from the blog postings, which included a few blocks not patterned in this book.

*Circle of Friends*, 84″ × 94″, coordinated and set by Becky Brown, Montpelier, Virginia; machine quilted by Deb Jacobs, 2011

Blog readers around the world made blocks for this quilt, a gift for Barbara Brackman in appreciation of the history lessons and quilt patterns that she posted each week throughout 2011 on her blog about Civil War quilts. Quilters became a circle of friends as they enjoyed the history, stitched their blocks, and shared them online through the Flickr group that Dustin Cecil created for the readers. Blocks arrived from Australia, Canada, France, Germany, Malaysia, the Netherlands, Portugal, and the United States.

The 7 × 8 format of 56 blocks includes some duplicates and several that are not included in the blog or the book. The sashing, with cornerstones, finishes to 2″ wide, as does the inner tan border. The mitered outer border finishes to 4″ wide (blue stripe and brown), cut from a large striped fabric, a good finish to a Civil War–era reproduction quilt.

I was born to blog—a skill I did not realize until recently. Throughout 2011, the 150th anniversary of the Civil War's commencement, I featured a weekly pattern to commemorate the sesquicentennial. I posted instructions for a traditional block with a short story about the war from a first-person account. I hoped a few readers might find it every Saturday morning and enjoy the women's perspective on history. A few might actually sew the blocks.

Within a few weeks, I had 100,000 hits. Apparently there was an audience for Civil War blocks and women's history.

By the end of the year, more than 1,000 people around the world had followed the blog, and many steadfast stitchers had made all the blocks. It was wonderful to hear from people in places such as Finland and South Africa, and to learn that a woman in Kuala Lumpur, Malaysia, was changing her market day from Saturday to Sunday so that she could log on to the blog. I found additional tasks: I tried to give a short answer to a woman in Germany who wondered why so much Northern/Southern sectionalism remains and to explain to several readers (brand new quilters, I bet) the difference between an 8″ × 8″ finished block and the 8½″ × 8½″ block they wound up with. I enjoyed helping friends mail swatches to each other across the oceans. I learned how to print a page from the Internet and explained it to someone in Brazil. And maybe the best gift of all was a surprise friendship quilt made by readers worldwide.

Dorsetspinner often posted her finished block pictured with one of her antique sewing machines, here a Wheeler & Wilson treadle.

Patchie13 in France thought that 8″ × 8″ blocks were too big, so she redrafted the patterns to 2″ × 2″ square. We were all delighted every week to see her tiny blocks contrasted with her thimble. (Note: No instructions are given for 2″ × 2″ blocks!)

I had help. Becky Brown stitched all the blocks and checked the directions a few weeks before I posted them. Dustin Cecil volunteered to manage a Flickr picture-sharing group where people could post their photos. (Becky and Dustin conspired with readers on the surprise quilt.) And I had help from new friends who posted their blocks every week—many of their online photos are in this book.

I chose the blocks in the book for their symbolic names. Most of them were published in the 1930s in the newspaper columns of the *Chicago Tribune* and the *Kansas City Star*, long after the war was over. Few of the blocks actually date from as long ago as 150 years, but I used the symbolism in the names to recall the war's events and the words of the witnesses. Add your own meaning with symbolic color, pictorial fabrics, and inked inscriptions, as many blog readers did.

The blog featured 8″ × 8″ blocks with a suggestion to make a quilt with all of them. For the book I've made some changes, adding instructions for 12″ × 12″ blocks. I didn't include patterns here that I'd offered in other Civil War books, and I substituted a few new stories and patterns to round out the 50. The blocks are renumbered here, and they are grouped for ease of stitching.

Enjoy the book. I hope you have as much fun reading it as I did writing that blog and realizing how worldwide the Web actually is.

The first thirteen blocks are all four-patches based on squares and triangles—good beginner blocks. The last two block patterns in this chapter are a little harder, but by then you should be able to make them. Some of the pattern pieces are interchangeable within the finished block size. Decide whether you want to make finished 8″ × 8″ squares or 12″ × 12″ squares, and follow these cutting instructions for the pieces in each block.

**NOTE:** The following pattern summary is used only in Chapter 1 as a tool for ease of constructing the blocks. Use your favorite method to make half-square triangle units and quarter-square triangle units, or cut out the triangles first and then stitch them together.

## 8″ × 8″ Blocks

**A:** Cut squares 2½″ × 2½″.

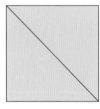

**B:** Cut squares 2⅞″ × 2⅞″. Cut each in half diagonally, creating 2 triangles.

**C:** Cut squares 4⅞″ × 4⅞″. Cut each in half diagonally, creating 2 triangles.

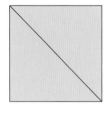

**D:** Cut squares 5¼″ × 5¼″. Cut each in half diagonally twice, creating 4 triangles.

**E:** Cut rectangles 2½″ × 4½″.

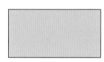

**F:** Cut squares 6⅞″ × 6⅞″. Cut each in half diagonally, creating 2 triangles.

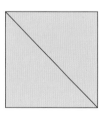

**G:** Cut squares 2⅛″ × 2⅛″. Cut each in half diagonally, creating 2 triangles.

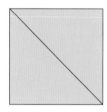

**H:** Cut squares 3½″ × 3½″. Cut each in half diagonally, creating 2 triangles.

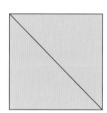

# 12″ × 12″ Blocks

**A:** Cut squares 3½″ × 3½″.

**B:** Cut squares 3⅞″ × 3⅞″. Cut each in half diagonally, creating 2 triangles.

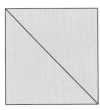

**C:** Cut squares 6⅞″ × 6⅞″. Cut each in half diagonally, creating 2 triangles.

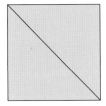

**D:** Cut squares 7¼″ × 7¼″. Cut each in half diagonally twice, creating 4 triangles.

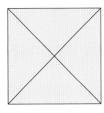

**E:** Cut rectangles 3½″ × 6½″.

**F:** Cut squares 9⅞″ × 9⅞″. Cut each in half diagonally, creating 2 triangles.

**G:** Cut squares 2⅞″ × 2⅞″. Cut each in half diagonally, creating 2 triangles.

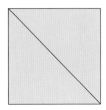

**H:** Cut squares 4⅞″ × 4⅞″. Cut each in half diagonally, creating 2 triangles.

# White House

Block by Country Log Cabin

Block by Liesbeth Wessels

*Courtesy of the Library of Congress*

The White House during the War

White House recalls Washington City, the Union capital perched on the edge of the Confederacy. During the War's first weeks, Washingtonians chose sides. Virginian Elizabeth Lindsay Lomax, who lived near the White House, gave a vivid account of the week the War began. Her youngest son, U.S. Army officer Lindsay Lomax, was a graduate of West Point. He and friend Jeb Magruder spent time at Elizabeth's house that week.

**April 16, 1861**
*Rained all night. Reported again last evening that Virginia has seceded, but it is not believed.*

**April 18**
*Virginia has seceded!! Heaven help us.*

**April 19**
*Visitors all day long. Many people are leaving the city. Great excitement and unrest.*

**April 21**
*This has been a frightfully exciting day. Riots here and in Baltimore, many persons shot, also a heartrending day for Lindsay and for me.… This evening Lindsay told me that he had sent in his resignation; Colonel Magruder has also sent in his resignation from the army and will go to Virginia tomorrow where Lindsay will join him.*

The first paragraph of Lindsay's letter:

*"I cannot stand it any longer and feel it my duty to resign. My State is out of the Union and when she calls for my services I feel that I must go. I regret it very much, realizing that the whole thing is suicidal."*

The White House pattern is a variation of a mid-twentieth-century block, designed by the *Chicago Tribune*'s Nancy Cabot in 1937.

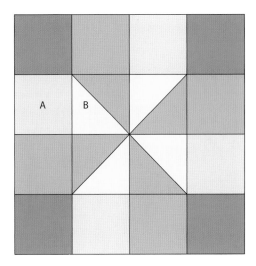

## Cutting

Refer to pattern piece sizes for 8″ × 8″ or 12″ × 12″ finished blocks (pages 6–7) and the blocks for your shading preferences. Cut the following:

**A:** 4 light, 4 medium, and 4 dark squares

**B:** 2 light and 2 medium squares cut to make 4 triangles of each

## Reference

*Lindsay Lomax Wood (editor), Leaves from an Old Washington Diary, 1854–1863 (New York: Dutton, 1943).*

Block by Becky Brown

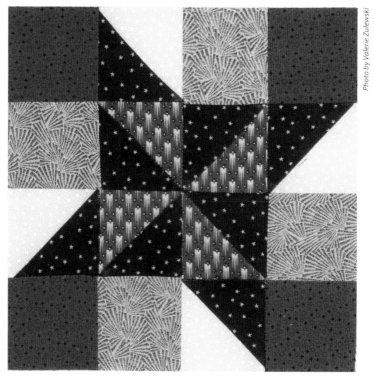

Block by Valerie Zulewski

Jessie Benton Frémont in the 1850s

Lincoln's recollection:

*"She sought an audience with me at midnight and taxed me so violently with many things that I had to exercise all the awkward tact I have to avoid quarreling with her."*

Jessie was out of place, a wife deputized to discuss policy. The meeting went badly, and so did Frémont's subsequent career. Lincoln removed him from the Missouri command. The War remained an official fight for the Union, not a fight against slavery—for the time being.

Star of the West is an old block also called Clay's Choice, a tribute to earlier politician Henry Clay, according to Ruth Finley in her 1929 book, *Old Patchwork Quilts and the Women Who Made Them.*

Star of the West symbolizes the first emancipation proclamation and mid-nineteenth-century power couple Jessie and John Frémont. In 1861 General Frémont was commander of the Union Army in Missouri, a state torn by conflicting loyalties. He declared martial law, warning that armed rebels would be court-martialed and shot, and their property confiscated. Their slaves "are hereby declared freemen."

Frémont's emancipation proclamation displeased President Lincoln, who warned: "Liberating slaves of traitorous owners will alarm our Southern Union friends and turn them against us." Frémont publicly refused to rescind his order, and Jessie went to Washington to argue their case. Her account:

*"The President said, 'You are quite a female politician.' I felt the sneering tone and saw there was a foregone decision against all listening. Then the President spoke more rapidly and unrestrainedly: 'The General ought not to have done it.... The General should never have dragged the Negro into the war. It is a war for a great national object and the Negro has nothing to do with it.'"*

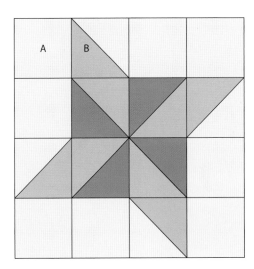

## Cutting

Refer to pattern piece sizes for 8″ × 8″ or 12″ × 12″ finished blocks (pages 6–7) and the blocks for your shading preferences. Cut the following:

**A:** 8 light squares

**B:** 2 light, 4 medium, and 2 dark squares cut to make 4 light, 8 medium, and 4 dark triangles

## Reference

*Mr. Lincoln's White House,*
*www.mrlincolnswhitehouse.org > Search "Frémont."*
*Accessed December 2011.*

*Photo by Amy E. Armstrong*

Block by Amy E. Armstrong

*Photo by Jo Schreiber*

Block by Jo Schreiber

Barbara Frietchie. Collectible photographs of the heroine were sold at Civil War fund-raising fairs.

Poetry was powerful propaganda during the Civil War. John Greenleaf Whittier, who often described current events in verse, heard a story about a Union heroine in a battle in Frederick, Maryland. His poem "Barbara Frietchie" became a rallying cry for the Union and a classic recitation for schoolchildren for generations.

Barbara Frietchie is recalled as an elderly woman who waved a Union flag from her attic while General Stonewall Jackson marched his Confederate troops through town. Jackson ordered his men to fire at the defiant woman.

> *"Shoot if you must, this old gray head,*
> *But spare your country's flag," she said.*

According to the poem, the embarrassed general rescinded the order and Frietchie's Union flag waved over Jackson's short occupation of the town. Historians point out that Stonewall Jackson, who died in battle soon after the poem's events, marched nowhere near Frietchie's house and that the 95-year-old woman was confined to bed.

Barbara Frietchie's defiant flag waving is an American myth flying in the face of the facts.

True or not, her tale was a Union answer to the Confederate myth of the martyr Jackson. Here was a woman who'd won a small victory over the legendary general.

In the 1930s, *Needlecraft Magazine* published an article about the re-creation of Frietchie's house in Maryland. On the bed: A sawtooth star, which "tradition assures us that Barbara made … with her own hands." *Needlecraft* pictured a block, naming it Barbara Frietchie's Design. We have here an imaginary story and an imaginary quilt block, but they remind us of the power of myth in telling about our past.

This version, made of 32 same-sized triangular pieces, was given the name Barbara Frietchie by the Grandmother Clark Needlework Company in 1932.

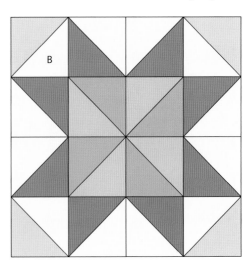

## Cutting

Refer to pattern piece sizes for 8″ × 8″ or 12″ × 12″ finished blocks (pages 6–7) and the blocks for your shading preferences. Cut the following:

**B:** 6 light, 2 medium light, 2 medium, 2 medium dark, and 4 dark squares cut to make 12 light, 4 medium light, 4 medium, 4 medium dark, and 8 dark triangles

*Photo by Amy E. Armstrong*

Block by Amy E. Armstrong

*Photo by Donna J. Keating*

Block by Donna J. Keating aka Quilting Bear Gal

The Washingtons placed advertisements in the newspapers of the day.

Catch Me If You Can recalls thousands of runaway slaves with one well-documented story. In 1796 Ona Judge left a ship in Portsmouth, New Hampshire. Just fifteen years old, the runaway slave hoped to pass as a free black in Portsmouth's small African-American community. Her owners wanted her back; she "was handy and useful ... being perfect Mistress of her needle." Under the 1793 Fugitive Slave Act, Portsmouth's officials were obliged to arrest her.

Ona's master was quite familiar with the Fugitive Slave Act. As President of the United States, he had signed it into law. Despite George Washington's position, New Hampshire officials released Ona, fearing a riot if they forcibly returned her to Virginia.

The Washingtons suggested other tactics, but their agent warned it would be difficult to persuade Ona and just as hard to kidnap her.

> "I am informed that many Slaves from the southern states have come to Massachusetts and some to New Hampshire, either of which States they consider as an asylum; the popular opinion here in favor of universal freedom has rendered it difficult to get them back to their masters."

Like many slaveholders, the Washingtons believed outsiders had stirred up discontent. Martha was of the opinion that a deranged Frenchman had seduced Ona. But the authorities who talked to Ona explained that escape was her own idea—her "thirst for compleat [sic] freedom ... had been her only motive for absconding."

Don't make the mistake of thinking this block with its charming name was code or communication on the Underground Railroad. Pattern writer Carrie Hall assigned the name in 1935 with no mention of slavery or the Civil War. We are free, however, to assign meaning in our own quilts, but don't assume earlier generations saw the same symbolism.

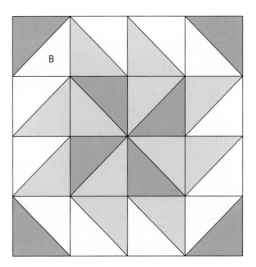

## Cutting

Refer to pattern piece sizes for 8″ × 8″ or 12″ × 12″ finished blocks (pages 6–7) and the blocks for your shading preferences. Cut the following:

**B:** 6 light, 6 medium, and 4 dark squares cut to make 12 light, 12 medium, and 8 dark triangles

## Reference

*Evelyn Gerson, Ona Judge Staines: Escape from Washington, www.seacoastnh.com > Search "Ona Judge Staines." Accessed December 2011.*

*Photo by Becky Brown*

Block by Becky Brown

*Photo by Leonie Weatherley*

Block by Leonie Weatherley

Guerilla raiders in Virginia, from *Harper's Weekly*

"Hawk" seems to have meant a thief of any kind. In 1861 Anne S. Frobel in northern Virginia instructed her slaves to bury the silver, a common precaution, exclaiming in her diary, "What spoonhawks these Yankees are!"

Hovering Hawks was given that name by Ruth Finley in 1929.

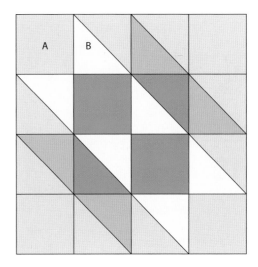

Hawks are predators that keep a hawk eye out for breakfast of smaller birds and rodents, so we can see how their name was appropriated for scavengers during the Civil War. Best known are the Jayhawks, or Jayhawkers, who swooped in during the prewar days of the Kansas troubles. When the war began, many blamed Jayhawkers for any and all raids. Roxanna Cole in North Carolina complained about a Colonel Lee and his Jayhawkers for local depredations:

> *"'Subsisting on the enemy' they call it. But they don't tell that they take the bread from women and children (for men are long since gone).... They came and demanded quilts and comforts. I told them that I had none that I could spare. They answered insolently that 'It makes no difference about that. Go and get two.' I almost cried that I had to give up my nice comforts to such swine and I had none but nice ones."*

## Cutting

Refer to pattern piece sizes for 8″ × 8″ or 12″ × 12″ finished blocks (pages 6–7) and the blocks for your shading preferences. Cut the following:

**A:** 4 medium light and 2 dark squares

**B:** 3 light, 4 medium light, 2 medium, and 1 dark square cut to make 6 light, 8 medium light, 4 medium, and 2 dark triangles

## References

*Thomas Felix Hickerson, Echoes of Happy Valley: Letters and Diaries (By the author, 1962).*

*M.H. and D.M. Lancaster (editors), The Civil War Diary of Anne S. Frobel (By the authors, 1986).*

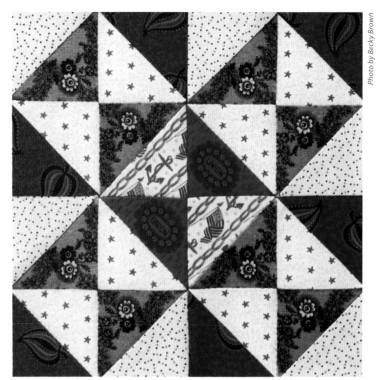

Block by Becky Brown

Block by Melissa L. Devin

Drawing of the Union Navy landing in the Carolinas, 1861, by Alfred R. Waud

A block with a seafaring name remembers the first impressive Northern victory when the Union captured Port Royal Sound in the Sea Islands near Charleston, South Carolina. Beaufort was the largest town in the swampy islands, with cotton plantations worked by thousands of slaves. Admiral Samuel Francis Du Pont's letters describe the first days of Union occupation:

> "You can form no idea of the terror we have spread in the whole Southern country. Beaufort is deserted…. The enemy flew in panic leaving public and private property, letters … clothes, arms, etc. The contrabands [freed slaves] are wild and sacking Beaufort, in return for being shot down because they would not leave with their masters. One called out in a broad grin … 'They thought you could not do it.'"

A week later Du Pont wrote:

> "The inhabitants fled not from fear of us but from the dread of their own Negroes; a few household servants followed their masters, but the field hands they dare not attempt to control, and the overseers had run with their masters. There are fifteen slaves to one white in this part; the [planters] threatened to shoot if they did not follow them into the interior, but I believe dare not attempt to execute this threat. The Negroes, anxious to show everything, said, 'Massa, they more afraid [of] us, than you'—this was often repeated…. The beautiful oleanders and chrysanthemums smiled on this scene of robbery and confusion."

Port and Starboard, pieced solely of half-square triangles, was given the nautical name in the *Chicago Tribune*'s Nancy Cabot column in 1937.

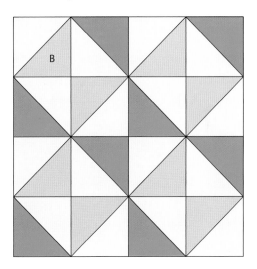

## Cutting

Refer to pattern piece sizes for 8″ × 8″ or 12″ × 12″ finished blocks (pages 6–7) and the blocks for your shading preferences. Cut the following:

**B:** 8 light, 4 medium, and 4 dark squares cut to make 16 light, 8 medium, and 8 dark triangles

## Reference

*John D. Hayes (editor), Samuel Francis Du Pont: A Selection from His Civil War Letters (Ithaca: Cornell University Press, 1969).*

*Photo by Roseanne Smith*

Block by Roseanne Smith

"Union and Liberty" reads the shield on this patriotic envelope from the Civil War years.

Confederate secession was not the first time a state or region had threatened disunion. Despite the first Articles of Confederation in 1777, Americans questioned whether different regions with different cultures and economic interests should be united. During the War of 1812, New England states gave serious consideration to breaking off from the Southern states, home of Jefferson and Madison, whom they blamed for the problems with England.

In 1808, immigrant Rosalie Stier Calvert wrote her father in Europe:

> "The eastern states complain loudly about
> the southern states. All this tends to make
> the condition of America as uncertain as that
> of Europe. For my part, I do not believe this
> government will long continue as it is now—
> the eastern and northern states will detach
> themselves and we will have a king in the south.
> That is my prophecy."

About 1830, Southern states decided they could nullify any federal laws not in their own self-interests. Southerner John C. Calhoun gave a famous toast, "The Union; second to our liberty most dear!" New Englander Daniel Webster followed with a speech that echoed through the Civil War years: "Liberty and Union, now and for ever, one and inseparable!"

In 1938 the Nancy Cabot quilt column in the *Chicago Tribune* gave this variation of an old pattern that also might be called Broken Dishes with the suggested red, white, and blue color scheme.

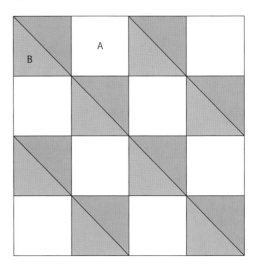

## Cutting

Refer to pattern piece sizes for 8″ × 8″ or 12″ × 12″ finished blocks (pages 6–7) and the block for your shading preferences. Cut the following:

**A:** 8 white squares

**B:** 4 red and 4 blue squares cut to make 8 red and 8 blue triangles

## Reference

*Margaret Law Callcott (editor), Mistress of Riversdale: The Plantation Letters of Rosalie Stier Calvert (Baltimore: Johns Hopkins University Press, 1992), p. 184.*

Block by Maria José Puente

Block by Ann Champion

Confederate flag over the ruins of Fort Sumter, 1861

Fox and Geese represents the standoff for Fort Sumter that led to the war's commencement. President Lincoln's first crisis focused on the Union fort in Charleston's harbor. Food was running out and South Carolinians threatened to fire upon any supply ships.

Gustavus Fox led Navy ships south in what he hoped would be a stealth mission, but he was outmaneuvered in this game of fox and geese. The Confederates assaulted the Union fort before the ships arrived, and federal soldiers abandoned Fort Sumter to the rebels.

On April 16, 1861, Sarah Espey of Alabama wrote in her diary:

> "A stormy day and getting cold … Thomas went to Hale's and learned that the Carolinians have taken Fort Sumter and that our other volunteer company is ordered to Fort-Pickens; so I suppose the war is now opened."

The Fox and Geese pattern is an old design given that name in Carrie Hall's 1935 index to patterns. We find variations of these four patches made of large and small triangles, but no record of what mid-nineteenth-century quilters might have called them.

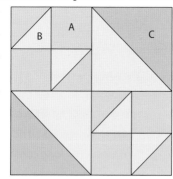

## Cutting

Refer to pattern piece sizes for 8″ × 8″ or 12″ × 12″ finished blocks (pages 6–7) and the blocks for your shading preferences. Cut the following:

**A:** 4 medium light squares

**B:** 2 light and 2 medium light squares cut to make 4 light and 4 medium light triangles

**C:** 1 light and 1 medium square cut to make 2 light and 2 medium triangles

## Reference

*Edward D.C. Campbell and Joan E. Cashin, A Woman's War: Southern Women, Civil War, and the Confederate Legacy (Richmond: Museum of the Confederacy, 1996), p. 74.*

*Home Again*, an 1866 lithograph, celebrates the end of the war.

Block by Barbara Brackman

Peace and Plenty is a two-part pattern: center and frame of two different sizes of triangles. Twentieth-century designers at *Farm Journal* magazine gave it a two-part name, like Corn and Beans or Hens and Chicks.

Post–Civil War orators often called for a reunified American peace and plenty. This biblical phrase was borrowed by Shakespeare. King Cymbeline's reunion with his sons, torn away by war, promised his country peace and plenty. A Scottish song published in 1776 carried the words into the New World as a symbol for reunion:

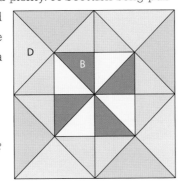

> "Lay your disputes all aside.... May peace and plenty be [our] lot."

## Cutting

Refer to pattern piece sizes for 8″ × 8″ or 12″ × 12″ finished blocks (pages 6–7) and the blocks for your shading preferences. Cut the following:

**B:** 2 light, 2 medium light, 2 medium, and 2 dark squares cut to make 4 triangles of each

**D:** 1 light and 1 medium square cut twice to make 4 light and 4 medium triangles

Block by Roseanne Smith

Block by Becky Brown

Block by Deb Henricks

Abraham Lincoln at the beginning of his presidency in 1862, by Mathew Brady

A few months later Lincoln signed the Emancipation Proclamation, freeing the slaves in the rebellious states and continuing the process of untangling the complex knot of slavery and union. Recall the conflict between Lincoln's official and personal views with an old block called Yankee Puzzle by Ruth Finley in her 1929 quilt book, *Old Patchwork Quilts and the Women Who Made Them.*

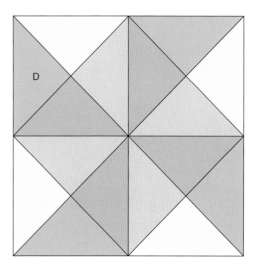

Yankee Puzzle recalls the basic problem with the Union's initial war philosophy: The Civil War was a war to maintain the Union—not to free the slaves. Abraham Lincoln explained the challenge in a letter to newspaper editor Horace Greeley (a lawyer's letter to be sure):

> *"If I could save the Union without freeing any slave I would do it, and if I could save it by freeing all the slaves I would do it; and if I could save it by freeing some and leaving others alone, I would also do that. What I do about slavery and the colored race, I do because I believe it helps to save [the] Union.… I have here stated my purpose according to my view of official duty; and I intend no modification of my oft-expressed personal wish that all men everywhere could be free."*

## Cutting

Refer to pattern piece sizes for 8″ × 8″ or 12″ × 12″ finished blocks (pages 6–7) and the blocks for your shading preferences. Cut the following:

**D:** 1 square each of 4 fabrics cut twice to make 4 triangles of each fabric

## Reference

*Edward McPherson, The Political History of the United States of America during the Great Rebellion (Washington: Philp & Solomons, 1865), p. 334.*

*Photo by Becky Brown*

Block by Becky Brown

*Photo by Helen McNaught*

Block by Helen McNaught

A Confederate blockade runner battles Union forces near Newport News.

Union strategy included a blockade of Southern ports along the ocean, gulf, and rivers in hopes that the Confederacy, with little manufacturing business, would surrender due to hardships. But Southern women took great pride in doing without. Parthenia Hague wrote a memoir about the shortages and substitutes. Here she writes about making homemade shoes:

*"Our shoes, particularly those of women and children, were made of cloth, or knit. Someone had learned to knit slippers, and it was not long before most of the women of our settlement had a pair of slippers on the knitting needles. They were knit of our homespun thread, either cotton or wool, which was, for slippers, generally dyed a dark brown, gray, or black. When taken off the needles, the slippers or shoes were lined with cloth of suitable texture. The upper edges were bound with strips of cloth, of color to blend with the hue of the knit work. A rosette was formed of some stray bits of ribbon, or scraps of fine bits of merino or silk, and placed on the uppers of the slippers; then they were ready for the soles....*

*"Sometimes we put on the soles ourselves by taking wornout shoes, whose soles were thought sufficiently strong to carry another pair of uppers, ripping the soles off, placing them in warm water to make them more pliable and to make it easier to pick out all the old stitches, and then in the same perforations stitching our knit slippers or cloth-made shoes."*

Recall Southern women's ingenuity with Blockade, redrawn from a design published in the *Kansas City Star* in 1938.

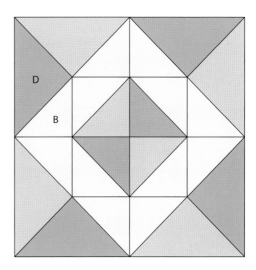

## Cutting

Refer to pattern piece sizes for 8″ × 8″ or 12″ × 12″ finished blocks (pages 6–7) and the blocks for your shading preferences. Cut the following:

**B:** 6 light, 1 medium, and 1 dark square cut to make 12 light, 2 medium, and 2 dark triangles

**D:** 1 medium and 1 dark square cut twice to make 4 medium and 4 dark triangles

---

*Hint for piecing*

*Join the D triangles in pairs; join the 4 B triangles together; then join the D units with the B units. Next, join the four-patch units together.*

---

### Reference

*Parthenia Antoinette Hague, A Blockaded Family: Life in Southern Alabama during the Civil War (Boston: Houghton Mifflin Company, 1888), pp. 53 and 54.*

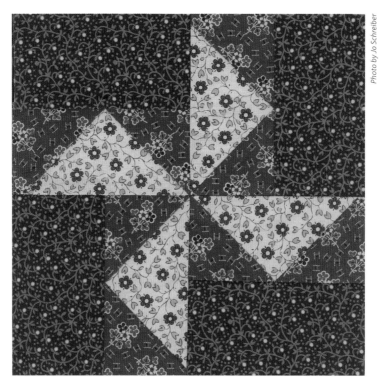

*Photo by Jo Schreiber*

Block by Jo Schreiber

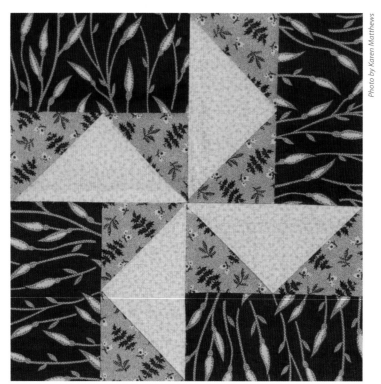

*Photo by Karen Matthews*

Block by Karen Matthews

Sarah Morgan

*broken open. Over it was spread all my letters, and private papers, a diary I kept when twelve years old, and sundry tokens of dried roses, etc., which must have been very funny, them all being labeled with the donor's name and the occasion. Fool! How I writhe when I think of all they saw.... Lilly's sewing-machine had disappeared; but as mother's was too heavy to move, they merely smashed the needles."*

The block was first published in *Hearth & Home* magazine about a century ago when the magazine asked readers to mail in patterns named for their home states.

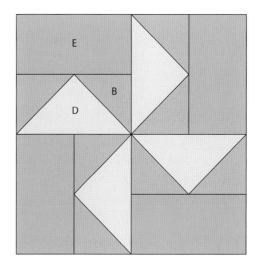

When Union armies overran Southern towns, families had to choose whether to leave or stay. Sarah Morgan, her mother, and her sisters spent much of the war as refugees from their home in Baton Rouge. Their house was severely damaged, not from battle but from vandalism by victorious Yankees. The women landed at a plantation twenty miles north of Baton Rouge, and sister Miriam returned from a trip to their battered neighborhood.

> *"She says when she entered [our] house, she burst into tears at the desolation. It was one scene of ruin. Libraries emptied, china smashed, sideboards split open with axes, three cedar chests cut open, plundered, and set up on end; all parlor ornaments carried off.... They entered my room, broke that fine mirror for sport, pulled down the rods from the bed and with them pulverized my toilet set, taking all Lydia's china ornaments I had packed in the wash-stand. The debris filled my basin and ornamented my bed. My desk was*

## Cutting

Refer to pattern piece sizes for 8″ × 8″ or 12″ × 12″ finished blocks (pages 6–7) and the blocks for your shading preferences. Cut the following:

**B:** 4 medium squares cut to make 8 triangles

**D:** 1 light square cut twice to make 4 triangles

**E:** 4 dark rectangles

## Reference

*Sarah Morgan Dawson, A Confederate Girl's Diary* (Boston: Houghton Mifflin Company, 1913), p. 191.

*Photo by Ernest Crawford*

Block by Barbara Crawford

*Photo by Carol Sanderson*

Block by Carol Sanderson

Fanny Kemble

London Square recalls Great Britain's role in the Civil War. England was our greatest trading partner and cotton was the currency. Many English supported the emerging Confederacy, but others were distressed at the prospect of an independent slave-based nation, among them actress Fanny Kemble.

Born into a London theatrical family, she became an American celebrity during an 1830 tour. Beautiful, bright, and spirited, she fell in love with Pierce Butler, who was temporarily living in Philadelphia. After their marriage, she accompanied him home to his Georgia rice plantations, where she discovered that the enormous Butler fortune was based on slavery. While there, she kept a detailed journal in the form of letters, recording slavery's horrible human toll.

Their marriage suffered from Fanny's attitudes about slavery and a woman's place, as well as from Pierce's neglect and bullying. In 1849 they obtained a very public divorce. Fanny lost custody of her daughters and gained a national reputation as a scandalous woman.

Back in England, where the Confederacy hoped to win recognition of its new state, Fanny realized she could use her fame and her writing skills to convince the English that the Southern cause was wrong. She published her *Journal of a Residence on a Georgia Plantation* in London in 1863, a shocking book that changed public opinion. England remained neutral.

*"I have sometimes been haunted with the idea that it was an imperative duty, knowing what I know, and having seen what I have seen, to do all that lies in my power to show the dangers and the evils of this frightful institution."*

London Square is a variation of the popular late-nineteenth-century design also called Ocean Waves. The name was published by the Famous Features Syndicate in the mid-twentieth century.

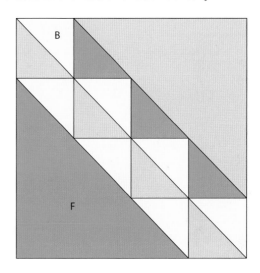

## Cutting

Refer to pattern piece sizes for 8″ × 8″ or 12″ × 12″ finished blocks (pages 6–7) and the blocks for your shading preferences. Cut the following:

**B:** 4 light, 2 medium, and 2 dark squares cut to make 8 light, 4 medium, and 4 dark triangles. Discard 1 light and 1 dark triangle.

**F:** 1 medium and 1 dark square cut to make 2 medium and 2 dark triangles. Discard 1 medium and 1 dark triangle.

## Reference

*Fanny Kemble, Records of Later Life (New York: Henry Holt & Company, 1883), p. 203.*

*Photo by Leonie Weatherley*

Block by Leonie Weatherley

*Photo by Ellen Murphy*

Block by Ellen Murphy from American Homestead

Courtesy of the Library of Congress

Rose Greenhow, about 1860

she met with England's prime minister and France's emperor, trying without success to persuade them to recognize the Confederate States of America. In London she published her autobiography, competing with Fanny Kemble for British loyalties.

Rose returned to America in 1864 with her publishing profits in gold coins hidden in a bag tied around her neck. The blockade-running ship carrying her into North Carolina ran aground. Rose was launched in a lifeboat that capsized. Weighted down by dispatches for Jefferson Davis and her fortune, she drowned in the Cape Fear River. Rosebud, given that name by the Ladies' Art Company about 1900, can remember the Confederacy's famous spy and diplomat.

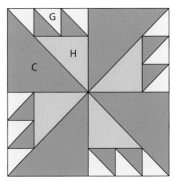

Washington socialite Rose Greenhow described in her autobiography how she spied on the Union Army during the war's first months.

> *"The 'grand army' was in motion, and I learned from a reliable source ... that the order for a forward movement had gone forth.... The tramp of armed men was heard on every side: martial music filled the air; in short, a mighty host was marshalling, with all the 'pomp and circumstance of glorious war.' 'On to Richmond!' was the war-cry."*

The Confederacy shocked North and South by beating that "grand army" in the first Battle of Manassas, keeping Richmond safe. Many credit or blame Rose, who was arrested a month later. Never one to hide her Confederate loyalties, she continued to pass information while she was held for two years without being charged. In 1863, she was exiled to the Confederate capital of Richmond and welcomed as a hero.

Confederate President Jefferson Davis appointed Rose an unofficial ambassador to Europe, where

## Cutting

Refer to pattern piece sizes for 8″ × 8″ or 12″ × 12″ finished blocks (pages 6–7) and the blocks for your shading preferences. Cut the following:

**C:** 2 dark squares cut to make 4 dark triangles

**G:** 6 light and 4 dark squares cut to make 12 light and 8 dark triangles

**H:** 2 medium squares cut to make 4 medium triangles

---

*Hint for piecing*

*Use a scant ¼″ seam allowance when joining the G triangles together and when joining them to the H triangles.*

---

## Reference

*Rose Greenhow, My Imprisonment and the First Year of Abolitionist Rule at Washington (London: Richard Bentley, 1863), pp. 14 and 15.*

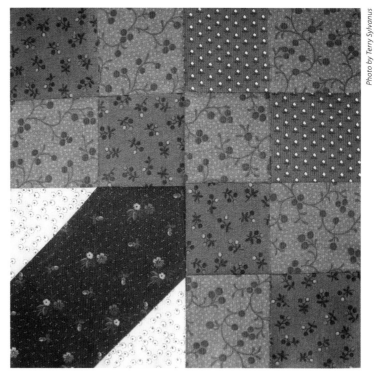

*Photo by Terry Sylvanus*

Block by Terry Sylvanus

*Photo by Becky Brown*

Block by Becky Brown

Jefferson Davis

Apple Tree can remind us of a Union song about Jefferson Davis, the only president of the Confederate States of America. He personified the Confederacy and its principles, whether one considered him hero or villain.

Union soldiers who'd been marching to the tune of "John Brown's Body" added lyrics to reflect their hatred of Davis with references to him and a sour apple tree. Sour apples might cause "the diah-ree" (diarrhea), which rhymed nicely with "tree." Or the branches could provide a scaffold for an on-the-spot execution if a Union soldier happened upon the very recognizable Davis.

*We'll hang Jeff Davis on a sour apple tree!*
*We'll hang Jeff Davis on a sour apple tree!*
*We'll hang Jeff Davis on a sour apple tree!*
*As we go marching on!*

Jeff Davis was not hanged. After the war he was released from federal prison after serving two years. This apple tree with red squares hanging in the green leaves was inspired by a block that Carrie Hall included in her 1935 book *Romance of the Patchwork Quilt*. Hall called it Tree of Temptation, a version of the biblical apple tree that caught Eve's eye. Here's a simpler apple tree.

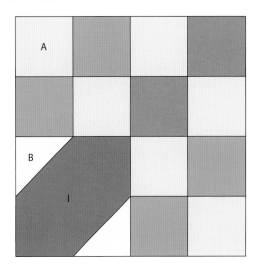

## Cutting

Refer to pattern piece sizes for 8″ × 8″ or 12″ × 12″ finished blocks (pages 6–7) and the blocks for your shading preferences. Cut the following:

**A:** 6 light, 4 dark green, and 2 red squares

**B:** 1 light square cut to make 2 light triangles

**I:** 1 dark rectangle 3⅜″ × 6⅜″ as part of an 8″ × 8″ block, or 4¾″ × 9⅛″ as part of a 12″ × 12″ block. Trim the edges of this rectangle at right angles as shown.

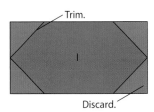

*Civil War Saturday Surprise*, 90″ × 100″, by Rosemary Youngs, Walker, Michigan; machine quilted by Tammy Finkler, 2011

Rosemary managed to keep up with the weekly blocks, making time between designing her own quilts for her new *Civil War Anniversary Quilt Book*, the third in her series of Civil War block books.

Her sashing of scrappy shirting prints (figures on white backgrounds) and corner-stones finishes to 2″ wide, framing 56 blocks in a 7 x 8 set. The striped border (almost a patchwork zigzag) finishes to 9″ wide.

The next six blocks are nine-patches based on equal divisions within the block. The nine-patch pattern pieces are interchangeable in these blocks. The last five patterns have uneven divisions. Decide if you want to make 8″ × 8″ blocks or 12″ × 12″ blocks and follow the cutting instructions for each pattern. The cut sizes for a 12″ × 12″ finished block are in parentheses.

Dancing the Virginia reel

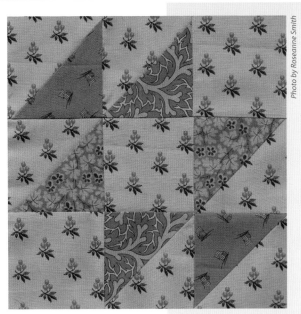

Block by Roseanne Smith

In June 1861, Tennessee was the last state to join the Confederacy, although the vote to secede didn't end the fight for Tennessee loyalties. Union and Confederate armies parried throughout the war, giving the state more battle sites than any but Virginia.

Leora "Babe" Sims saw the beginning of it all through a careless girl's eyes.

> *"Isn't our sucess [sic] miraculous?" she wrote a friend. "Memphis is a perfect camp ground. I think there could be as many as 20,000 troops here now.… We often ride out to see them and they look so picturesque. The soldiers are all so polite and gentlemanly.… The Tennesseans all love fighting.… I declare the rotten Yankees are too determined. Why don't they behave themselves and quit this war?"*

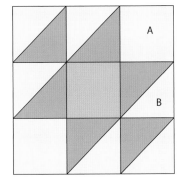

## Cutting

Refer to the blocks for your shading preferences. Decide whether you want an 8″ × 8″ block or a 12″ × 12″ block (12″ × 12″ block measurements are in parentheses). Cut the following:

Block by Barbara Brackman

**A:** 2 light and 1 medium square 3⅛″ × 3⅛″ (4½″ × 4½″)

**B:** 3 light and 3 dark squares 3½″ × 3½″ (4⅞″ × 4⅞″). Cut each in half diagonally to make 6 light and 6 dark triangles.

> ### Hint for piecing
> *Use scant ¼″ seam allowances when joining the square nine-patch units together to make a finished 8″ × 8″ block.*

## Reference

*Louis Palmer Towles (editor), A World Turned Upside Down: The Palmers of South Santee, 1818–1881 (Columbia: University of South Carolina Press, 1996), pp. 313 and 314.*

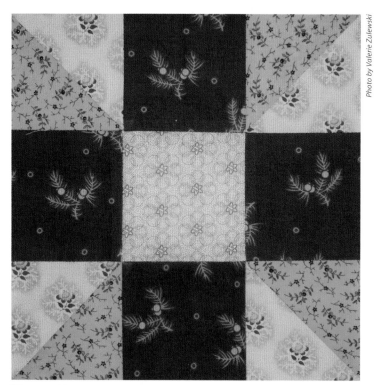

Block by Valerie Zulewski

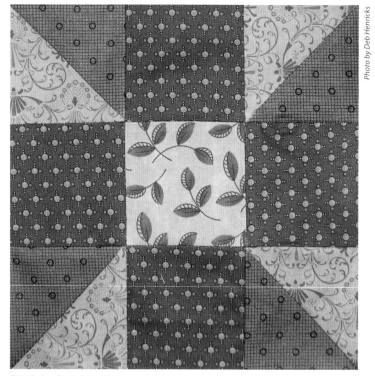

Block by Deb Henricks

Spring fashion that Clara could only dream about

During the war's first year, Clara Solomon began a diary. One of six daughters of a New Orleans dry goods merchant, sixteen-year-old Clara recorded her reactions to the Yankee occupation, her father's absence in the Confederate Army, and her family's increasing poverty. She wrote in the slang of her day, revealing that teenagers 150 years ago had their own language, some of which lingers. Her friend Alice "looked particularly 'jimmy' in a clean muslin.… Alice, I often think of you. Ain't that cool?"

By fall she was complaining about the price of cotton. "Former bit calicoes are now 20 and 25 cents.… What will the people do?"

Twenty-five cents is two bits, so the price of prints had doubled. Like most teenagers, she found "pretty dresses" a major concern:

*"Remained sewing until [2:30] when I proceeded to adorn my person. Wore my new dress with which I am in love."*

But wartime fabric costs broke her heart.

*"After School I came directly home. Ma was down stairs sewing.… [F] cautioned me not to go on Canal St. for I would see too much grand dressing for my own comfort. Innocent child! How often have I returned home almost downhearted at the remembrance of the pretty dresses and faces I had seen."*

We can remember Clara and fabric shortages with the Calico Puzzle block, first called by that name in the *Kansas City Star* in 1930.

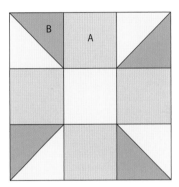

## Cutting

Refer to the blocks for your shading preferences. Decide whether you want an 8″ × 8″ block or a 12″ × 12″ block (12″ × 12″ block measurements are in parentheses). Cut the following:

**A:** 1 light and 4 medium squares 3⅛″ × 3⅛″ (4½″ × 4½″)

**B:** 2 light and 2 dark squares 3½″ × 3½″ (4⅞″ × 4⅞″). Cut each in half diagonally to make 4 light and 4 dark triangles.

> ### Hint for piecing
> *Use scant ¼″ seam allowances when joining the nine-patch units together to make an 8″ × 8″ block.*

## Reference

*Elliott Ashkenazi (editor), The Civil War Diary of Clara Solomon: Growing Up in New Orleans, 1861–1862 (Baton Rouge: Louisiana State University Press, 1995).*

*Photo by Becky Brown*

Block by Becky Brown

*Photo by Dustin Cecil*

Block by Dustin Cecil

Sassafras leaves also make filé, as in filé gumbo.

Sassafras tea made from roots and bark has long been a home-brewed staple. It's the traditional flavor in root beer and so much a Southern tradition that a reference to "cinnamon seed," or sassafras tea, is found in older versions of the song "Dixie," the unofficial Confederate anthem.

"Dixie" was probably a folk tune sung for decades before being published as a commercial minstrel song in 1859. The lively melody was popular in the North and was a favorite of Lincoln, but during the war "Dixie" became a Southern marching song.

The chorus is generally considered to be:

*Oh, I wish I was in the land of cotton,*
*Old times there are not forgotten,*
*Look away, look away, look away Dixie Land.*

Other versions substitute a reference to sassafras tea and catfish fishing in the second line:

*Oh, I wish I was in the land of cotton,*
*Cinnamon seed and sandy bottom,*
*Look away, look away, look away Dixie Land.*

Soldiers on both sides invented numerous versions. As the word "Dixie" increasingly became a nickname for the South, patriotic versions were published, such as this 1861 "Dixie War Song":

*Southrons, hear your country call you,*
*Up, lest worse than death befall you!*
*To arms! To arms! To arms, in Dixie!*

The Tea Leaf block can remind us of the song "Dixie" and Confederate tea substitutes during the blockade. It's one of many variations of this nine-patch. Pattern designers also saw it as a poplar, a magnolia, or a maple leaf.

## Cutting

Refer to the blocks for your shading preferences. Decide whether you want an 8″ × 8″ block or a 12″ × 12″ block (12″ × 12″ block measurements are in parentheses). Cut the following:

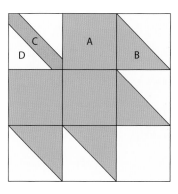

**A:** 1 light and 3 dark squares 3⅛″ × 3⅛″ (4½″ × 4½″)

**B:** 2 light and 2 dark squares 3½″ × 3½″ (4⅞″ × 4⅞″). Cut each in half diagonally to make 4 light and 4 dark triangles.

**C:** 1 medium rectangle 1″ × 4½″ (1¼″ × 6⅜″)

**D:** 1 light square 3⅛″ × 3⅛″ (4⅜″ × 4⅜″). Cut in half diagonally, creating 2 light triangles.

### Hints for piecing

- *Center rectangle C on the D edges when joining. Trim to square up.*

- *Use scant ¼″ seam allowances when joining the nine-patch units together to make a finished 8″ × 8″ block.*

### Reference

*Irwin Silber and Jerry Silverman, Songs of the Civil War (N. Chemsford, Massachusetts: Courier Dover Publications, 1995), p. 51.*

*Photo by Donna J. Keating*

Block by Donna J. Keating aka Quilting Bear Gal

*Photo by Ann Champion*

Block by Ann Champion

*Courtesy of the Library of Congress*

The town of Harpers Ferry

John Brown was hanged in 1859 for attacking a federal arsenal in Harpers Ferry, an insurrection that fired partisanship. Arguments continue about whether he was martyr or terrorist, but few remember the others who died in his "holy war."

Brown recruited antislavery soldiers in Oberlin, Ohio, an oasis of free thinking with a college open to women and African Americans. Black leader Charles Langston refused to accompany Brown, but two young men agreed to rendezvous for the attack. Lewis Sheridan Leary left his wife, Mary, home with a baby, telling her he was traveling on business.

The U.S. Army easily defeated Brown's tiny band. With bullets flying, Leary jumped into the Shenandoah. A nineteenth-century account follows:

> "A wretch, mortally wounded, was dragged from the river by a citizen, and laid upon the bank shivering with cold and loss of blood. He begged to be taken to a fire, promising to confess everything. The bystanders carried him to an old cooper's shop hardby, where a hasty blaze was kindled.… He entreated someone to write [his family] to inform them of the manner of his death.… After lingering in great agony for twelve hours he died."

Mary later told her grandson that weeks after Leary's death, his bullet-torn shawl arrived. That grandson, poet Langston Hughes, remembered sleeping under the plaid shawl as a boy. After the war, Mary married Charles Langston and gave birth to a son and a daughter, Langston Hughes's mother. Langston Hughes remembered Mary holding him and telling him tales in which "life moved heroically toward an

end.… Nobody ever cried in my grandmother's stories. They worked, or schemed, or fought. But no crying."

We can remember Oberlin's Learys and Langstons with Ohio Star.

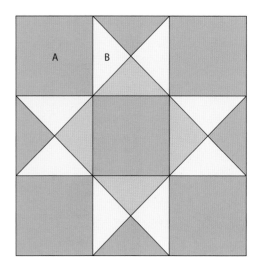

## Cutting

Refer to the blocks for your shading preferences. Decide whether you want an 8″ × 8″ block or a 12″ × 12″ block (12″ × 12″ block measurements are in parentheses). Cut the following:

**A:** 5 dark squares 3⅛″ × 3⅛″ (4½″ × 4½″)

**B:** 2 light, 1 medium, and 1 dark square 3⅞″ × 3⅞″ (5¼″ × 5¼″). Cut in half diagonally twice, creating 8 light, 4 medium, and 4 dark triangles.

---

### Hint for piecing

*Use scant ¼″ seam allowances when joining the nine-patch units together to make a finished 8″ × 8″ block.*

---

## References

*John Warner Barber and Henry Howe, Our Whole Country: Or the Past and Present of the United States, Historical and Descriptive (New York: Tuttle & McCauley, 1861), p. 649.*

*Langston Hughes, The Big Sea: An Autobiography (New York: Knopf, 1945), p. 17.*

*Photo by Karen Matthews*

Block by Karen Matthews

*Photo by Kathie Coombs*

Block by Kathie Coombs

Charles Bowditch was lucky enough to sit very near the presidential platform on the steps of the Capitol.

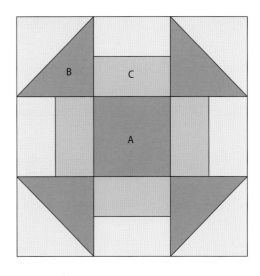

Charles Bowditch traveled to Washington for Abraham Lincoln's first presidential inauguration and documented his trip in letters to his mother back in Boston. Thanks to family connections he was invited *"to the Presidents [sic] rooms and found a good many people there consisting however, I believe of his and his wife's relations.… Mrs. Lincoln is a very pleasant looking woman and is by no means coarse looking as has been said. She was dressed in a brown silk with a black velvet cloak and a green plush bonnet."*

Charles was swept up with the Lincoln–Todd party and observed the ceremony with the family:

*"About 1 o'clock we went out to the front of the Capitol the steps of which had been floored over and took our seat. We then saw Messrs. Lincoln and Buchanan come down the steps and the Judges of the Supreme Court. Lincoln then delivered his inaugural amid much cheering and shouting and afterwards took his oath of office.… Thus you see the Inauguration has gone through very successfully and safely and Mr. Lincoln has not been made the victim of any hostile inventions or infernal machines [bombs].… Mr. Lincoln has rec'd a great many threatening letters which of course made the family feel very uncomfortably."*

This quilt pattern, which dates to the end of the nineteenth century, has many names, among them Shoo-Fly, Monkey Wrench, and Hole in the Barn Door. In her 1935 book, Carrie Hall called it Lincoln's Platform. Another war-related name is Sherman's March, first published by *Capper's Weekly* newspaper about the same time.

## Cutting

Refer to the blocks for your shading preferences. Decide whether you want an 8″ × 8″ block or a 12″ × 12″ block (12″ × 12″ block measurements are in parentheses). Cut the following:

**A:** 1 dark center square 3⅛″ × 3⅛″ (4½″ × 4½″)

**B:** 2 light and 2 dark squares 3½″ × 3½″ (4⅞″ × 4⅞″). Cut each in half diagonally to make 4 light and 4 dark triangles.

**C:** 4 light and 4 medium rectangles 1⅞″ × 3⅛″ (2½″ × 4½″)

---

### *Hints for piecing*

■ *After joining a pair of C rectangles, trim the unit to 3⅛″ × 3⅛″ when making an 8″ × 8″ block.*

■ *Use scant ¼″ seam allowances when joining the nine-patch units together to make a finished 8″ × 8″ block.*

---

### Reference

*Katherine W. Richardson, "'We Had a Very Fine Day': Charles Bowditch Attends Lincoln's Inauguration," in Essex Institute Historical Collections, Volume 124, Number 1, January 1988, pp. 28–35.*

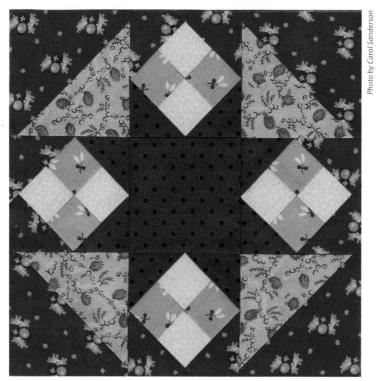

Photo by Carol Sanderson

Block by Carol Sanderson

Photo by Melissa L. Devin

Block by Melissa L. Devin

Varina Howell Davis as First Lady
of the Confederacy

Richmond was a capital of the Confederacy and home to Confederate President Jefferson Davis and his wife Varina Howell Davis. At the start of the war, their family included three children: Margaret, Jefferson, and Joseph.

Varina's wit and style are reflected in the diary of her close friend Mary Chesnut.

> *"Lunched, at Mrs. Davis's…. Mrs. Davis was as nice as the luncheon. When she is in the mood, I do not know so pleasant a person. She is awfully clever, always."*

War changed the lively young woman. Like her Union counterpart, Mary Lincoln, Varina Davis lost a child during the war. She recalled that day in 1864:

> *"I left my children quite well, playing in my room, and had just uncovered my [sewing] basket in [Jefferson's] office when a servant came in for me. The most beautiful and brightest of my children, Joseph Emory, had in play climbed over the connecting angle of the banister and fallen to the brick pavement below. He died a few minutes after we reached his side."*

She gave birth to her youngest that year and wrote to Mary Chesnut.

> *"Do come to me, and see how we get on.… Perfect bliss have I. The baby, who grows fat and is*

*smiling always, is christened, and not old enough to develop the world's vices or to be snubbed by it. The name so long delayed is Varina Anne. My name is a heritage of woe."*

The Richmond block was published about 1915 by *Hearth & Home* magazine, which asked readers for patchwork patterns for state capitals.

## Cutting

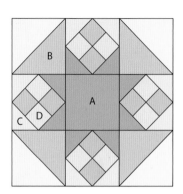

Refer to the blocks for your shading preferences. Decide whether you want an 8″ × 8″ block or a 12″ × 12″ block (12″ × 12″ block measurements are in parentheses). Cut the following:

**A:** 1 dark square 3⅛″ × 3⅛″ (4½″ × 4½″)

**B:** 2 medium light and 2 medium dark squares 3½″ × 3½″ (4⅞″ × 4⅞″). Cut each in half diagonally to make 4 medium light and 4 medium dark triangles.

**C:** 4 medium and 4 dark squares 2⅛″ × 2⅛″ (2⅞″ × 2⅞″). Cut each in half diagonally, creating 8 medium and 8 dark triangles.

**D:** 8 medium and 8 light squares 1½″ × 1½″ (1⅞″ × 1⅞″)

---

*Hint for piecing*

*Use scant ¼″ seam allowances when joining the square nine-patch units together to make a finished 8″ × 8″ block.*

---

## References

*Armistead Churchill Gordon, Jefferson Davis (New York: Charles Scribner's, 1918), pp. 227 and 228.*

*C. Vann Woodward (editor), Mary Chesnut's Civil War (New Haven: Yale University Press, 1993), pp. 62 and 786.*

Block by Barbara Brackman

*Photo by Roseanne Smith*

Block by Roseanne Smith

Shopping for small things like pins was only a rosy memory for many Southern women during the war.

Pins and needles were tiny manufactured items that became as much a rarity as yardage for a new dress in the Confederacy. Vandalizing troops broke needles on sewing machines, knowing there were no spares. Blockade runners and smugglers were the only source for expensive packets of English needles and wheels of glass-head pins, which were used for barter.

"A refugee" in Louisiana recalled a happy day in her new home state in late 1862. Her husband had bought the contents of a shuttered store and opened it to the neighbors.

*"Just imagine a lot of women without sewing materials of any kind!—No thread, no needles, buttons, etc., to say nothing of dress materials— turned loose in a country store.… We were overjoyed when we found about 60 yards of old- fashioned plaid barege, and such a plaid! The size of the squares and odd mixture of colors were very startling, but that made no difference. We rose above such small matters, it meant a dress."*

She was referring to the wild challis prints of the 1840s and 50s, ten years or more out of date. Pinwheel, given that name by Ruth Finley in 1929, recalls the days when pin money was useless and there was no such thing as an out-of-fashion fabric.

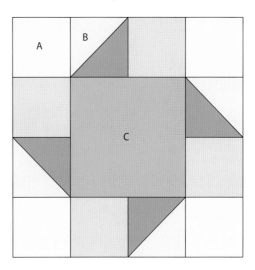

## Cutting

Refer to the blocks for your shading preferences. Decide whether you want an 8″ × 8″ block or a 12″ × 12″ block (12″ × 12″ block measurements are in parentheses). Cut the following:

**A:** 4 medium light and 4 medium squares 2½″ × 2½″ (3½″ × 3½″)

**B:** 2 light and 2 dark squares 2⅞″ × 2⅞″ (3⅞″ × 3⅞″). Cut each in half diagonally, creating 4 light and 4 dark triangles.

**C:** 1 medium dark square 4½″ × 4½″ (6½″ × 6½″)

### Reference

*Frances Hewitt Fearn (editor), Diary of a Refugee (New York: Moffat, Yard & Company, 1910), p. 22.*

*Photo by Amy E. Armstrong*

Block by Amy E. Armstrong

*Photo by Becky Brown*

Block by Becky Brown

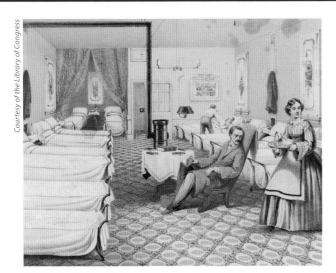

Courtesy of the Library of Congress

A Philadelphia hospital

Dix's reputation suffered from the backlash of ridicule that often results from a woman's assuming a position of power, but her efforts to break new ground for women saved many soldiers' lives.

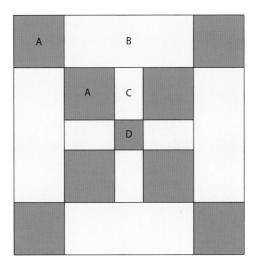

The Comfort Quilt pattern, given that name by the *Kansas City Star* in 1940, has two meanings. The patchwork imitates a woven comforter pattern, and bedcoverings were often called comforts. The design also recalls Dorothea Dix and Civil War nurses who comforted the wounded and ill.

Despite beliefs that women did not belong in hospitals, Dix recruited thousands to nurse Union soldiers.

Her criteria:

*No women under thirty need apply to serve in government hospitals.*

*All nurses are required to be plain looking women.*

*Their dresses must be brown or black with no bows, no curls, no jewelry and no hoop skirts.*

New Yorker Charlotte Wilson heard of nurse recruitment and the rules:

*"Miss Dolly Dix ... informs them of the wants of the Washington Hospital.... One of the first questions asked a woman who is ambitious to become a Nurse is whether she is over thirty. None under that age are accepted. It is wonderful how many find it impossible to confess they are over thirty."*

## Cutting

Refer to the blocks for your shading preferences. Decide whether you want an 8″ × 8″ block or a 12″ × 12″ block (12″ × 12″ block measurements are in parentheses). Cut the following:

**A:** 8 dark squares 2¼″ × 2¼″ (3⅛″ × 3⅛″)

**B:** 4 light rectangles 2¼″ × 5″ (3⅛″ × 7¼″)

**C:** 4 light rectangles 1½″ × 2¼″ (2″ × 3⅛″)

**D:** 1 dark square 1½″ × 1½″ (2″ × 2″)

## References

*Barbara Brackman, Civil War Women (Lafayette, California: C&T Publishing, 2000), p. 62.*

*Nancy Coffey Heffernan and Ann Page Stecker (editors), Sisters of Fortune (Hanover, New Hampshire: University Press of New England, 1993), p. 261.*

*Photo by Sue de Kam*

Block by Sue de Kam

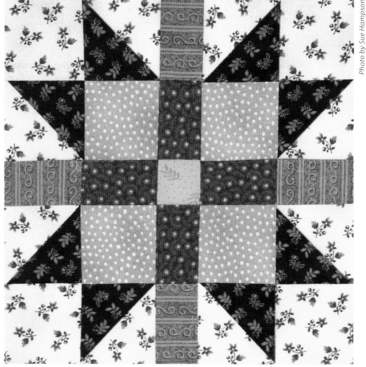

*Photo by Sue Hampson*

Block by Sue Hampson

Louisa May Alcott

The New England Block is a variation of a star that has been given several names over the last hundred years, this one assigned by a 1930s pattern company called Needlecraft Supply.

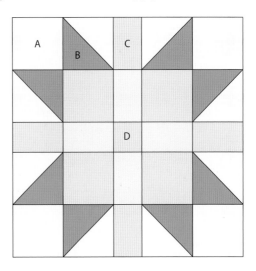

The New England Block can remind us of Louisa May Alcott. In 1861 this restless 28-year-old was living with her family in a ramshackle house in Concord, Massachusetts. She wrote an old friend that she was "sewing violently on patriotic blue shirts," despite her feelings toward needlework ("an abomination"). She wasn't alone in her patriotism.

> "The town is [in] a high state of topsey-turveyness, for every-one is boiling over with excitement and when quiet Concord does get stirred up it is a sight to behold. All the young men and boys drill with all their might, the women and girls sew and prepare for nurses, the old folks settle the fate of the Nation in groves of newspapers, and the children make the streets hideous with distracted drums and fifes. Everyone wears cockades wherever one can be stuck. Flags flap over head like parti-colored birds of prey, patriotic balmorals [jackets], cravats [ties], handkerchiefs and hats are all the rig, and if we keep on at our present rate everything in heaven and earth will soon be confined to red white and blue."

## Cutting

Refer to the blocks for your shading preferences. Decide whether you want an 8″ × 8″ block or a 12″ × 12″ block (12″ × 12″ block measurements are in parentheses). Cut the following:

**A:** 4 light and 4 medium squares 2¼″ × 2¼″ (3⅛″ × 3⅛″)

**B:** 4 light and 4 dark squares 2⅝″ × 2⅝″ (3½″ × 3½″). Cut each in half diagonally, creating 8 light and 8 dark triangles.

**C:** 4 medium and 4 medium dark rectangles 1½″ × 2¼″ (2″ × 3⅛″)

**D:** 1 medium square 1½″ × 1½″ (2″ × 2″)

## Reference

*Joel Myerson and Daniel Shealy (editors), The Selected Letters of Louisa May Alcott (Athens: University of Georgia Press, 1995), p. 64.*

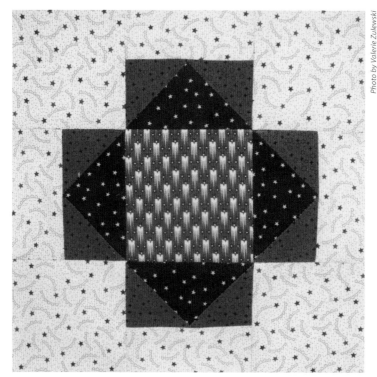

*Photo by Valerie Zulewski*

Block by Valerie Zulewski

*Photo by Becky Brown*

Block by Becky Brown

Photo by James Gardner. Courtesy of the Library of Congress

Women from the Sanitary Commission in Fredericksburg, Virginia, 1864. The barrels and boxes were often full of quilts.

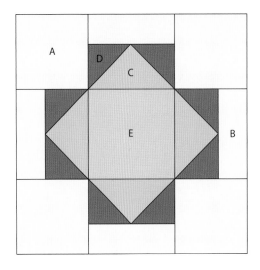

The Ladies' Aid Album honors the U.S. Sanitary Commission. If you see a shadow of a red cross, it's because the Sanitary Commission preceded the Red Cross in aiding sick and wounded soldiers. It surprises us that 150 years ago governments took little responsibility for war wounded. In Europe's Crimean War of the 1850s, Florence Nightingale established a civilian mission that saved many lives. Inspired by her work, the first Sanitary Commission grew as a civilian group authorized by the Union to take responsibility for soldiers' hospitals and medical care.

Cities all over the Northern states soon volunteered to organize local branches. One major duty was collecting blankets, medical supplies, food, and clothing for hospitals. Another was sewing those blankets, supplies, and clothing in numerous Ladies' Aid Societies. The Ladies' Aid Album block was published in the *Kansas City Star* in 1938. Here the design is redrawn to better fit an 8″ block.

## Cutting

Refer to the blocks for your shading preferences. Decide whether you want an 8″ × 8″ block or a 12″ × 12″ block (12″ × 12″ block measurements are in parentheses). Cut the following:

**A:** 4 light squares 3″ × 3″ (4¼″ × 4¼″)

**B:** 4 light rectangles 1½″ × 3½″ (2″ × 5″)

**C:** 1 medium square 4¼″ × 4¼″ (5¾″ × 5¾″). Cut in half diagonally twice, creating 4 medium triangles.

**D:** 4 red squares 2⅜″ × 2⅜″ (3⅛″ × 3⅛″). Cut each in half diagonally, creating 8 red triangles.

**E:** 1 medium square 3½″ × 3½″ (5″ × 5″)

Photo by Roseanne Smith

Block by Roseanne Smith

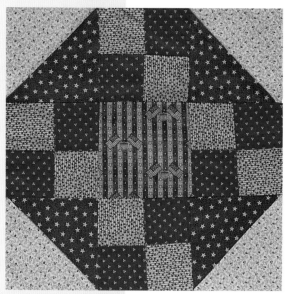

Block by Barbara Brackman

Taking the oath in occupied New Orleans

We remember the war in blue and gray. The colors symbolize Union versus Confederate, Yankee versus Rebel. John Thompson wrote of marching with the Rhode Island Volunteers through Virginia, where the Yankees found "many houses where meals could be had for a reasonable consideration, an opportunity which officers and men were not slow to improve [take advantage of]. At some places the families were true blue, and at others they had taken the oath of allegiance and were 'blue' without the true."

The oath involved swearing allegiance to the Union and the Constitution. In Union-occupied areas, those who refused to take the oath were barred from working, from receiving rations, and from shopping in stores, and many were jailed. Southerners swallowed their pride and turned "blue without the true." *Hearth & Home* magazine gave the name True Blue to this nine-patch in the early twentieth century.

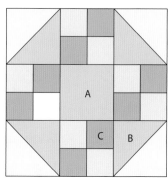

## Cutting

Refer to the blocks for your shading preferences. Decide whether you want an 8″ × 8″ block or a 12″ × 12″ block (12″ × 12″ block measurements are in parentheses). Cut the following:

**A:** 1 medium square 3⅛″ × 3⅛″ (4½″ × 4½″)

**B:** 2 light and 2 medium squares 3½″ × 3½″ (4⅞″ × 4⅞″). Cut each in half diagonally to make 4 light and 4 medium triangles.

**C:** 8 light and 8 dark squares 1⅞″ × 1⅞″ (2½″ × 2½″)

### Hints for piecing

■ *After piecing, trim the C-squares unit to 3⅛″ × 3⅛″ for the finished 8″ × 8″ block.*

■ *Use scant ¼″ seam allowances when joining the nine-patch units together to make a finished 8″ × 8″ block.*

## Reference

*John C. Thompson, History of the Eleventh Regiment, Rhode Island Volunteers (Providence: By the author, 1881), p. 56.*

The blocks in this chapter fall outside the simple four-patch or nine-patch format. They require some cutting and piecing skills that go a bit beyond the basics. Decide whether you want to make 8″ × 8″ blocks or 12″ × 12″ blocks and follow the cutting instructions for each pattern. The cut sizes for a 12″ × 12″ finished block are in parentheses.

Block by Barbara Brackman

Portrait of a boy soldier

Thomas Nelson Page in *Two Little Confederates* painted a picture of the limited treats available during the war. It may be fiction, but it's an accurate account of imported sugar shortages:

*"There was no sugar nor coffee nor tea. These luxuries had been given up long before. An attempt was made to manufacture sugar out of the sorghum, or sugar cane, which was now being cultivated as an experiment; but it proved unsuccessful, and molasses made from the cane was the only sweetening. The boys, however, never liked anything sweetened with molasses."*

We can think of the block, first published in 1932 in an agricultural newspaper, the *Rural New Yorker*, as an empty sugar bowl, just one of many deprivations children faced.

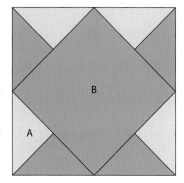

Block by Roseanne Smith

## Cutting

Refer to the blocks for your shading preferences. Decide whether you want an 8″ × 8″ block or a 12″ × 12″ block (12″ × 12″ block measurements are in parentheses). Cut the following:

**A:** 1 medium and 1 dark square 5¼″ × 5¼″ (7¼″ × 7¼″). Cut each in half diagonally twice, creating 4 medium and 4 dark triangles.

**B:** 1 dark square 6⅛″ × 6⅛″ (9″ × 9″)

### Reference

*Thomas Nelson Page, Two Little Confederates (New York: Scribner's, 1888), p. 47.*

Block by Barbara Brackman

*Photo by Roseanne Smith*

Block by Roseanne Smith

A Sanitary Commission convalescent hospital in Alexandria. Donated quilts would warm the beds here.

*Description of Articles Most Wanted:*
*Blankets for single beds*
*Quilts of cheap material …*

**—From an appeal by the**
**U.S. Sanitary Commission, 1861**

Here's a simple nine-patch within a frame to represent a particular type of quilt used by soldier's aid sewing societies during the war. Rather than making blocks and assembling them into a top to be quilted, individuals pieced, backed, quilted, and bound each block. The bound squares were then joined with a tight whipstitch into a bed-size quilt. Each square thus had a small frame of binding showing.

In research for an American Quilt Study Group paper, Pamela Weeks counted twelve surviving examples of quilts made to comfort soldiers or to raise money for Union soldiers' aid organizations. She noted that a majority were made using the bound block technique that we call potholder quilts or "quilt-as-you-go."

The binding was often a contrasting color, sometimes white. I've used a light blue. Roseanne used a mitered stripe as her frame. The frame here is symbolic, but you could think about doing a "quilt-as-you-go" technique for your sampler. My advice, having tried it two or three times: That's a lot of whipstitching! I'd rather quilt at the end.

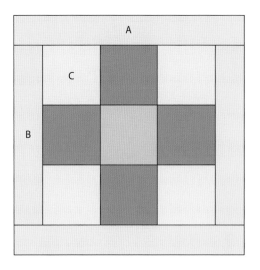

## Cutting

Refer to the blocks for your shading preferences. Decide whether you want an 8″ × 8″ block or a 12″ × 12″ block (12″ × 12″ block measurements are in parentheses). Cut the following:

**A:** 2 medium rectangles 1½″ × 8½″ (2″ × 12½″)

**B:** 2 medium rectangles 1½″ × 6½″ (2″ × 9½″)

**C:** 4 light, 1 medium, and 4 dark squares 2½″ × 2½″ (3½″ × 3½″)

## Reference

*Pamela Weeks, "One Foot Square, Quilted and Bound: A Study of Potholder Quilts," in Uncoverings 2010 (Lincoln: American Quilt Study Group, 2010), pp. 131–160.*

*Photo by Ernest Crawford*

Block by Barbara Crawford

*Photo by Liesbeth Wessels*

Block by Liesbeth Wessels

Harriet Beecher Stowe's characters, such as Simon Legree, the villainous overseer, became American classics.

The Log Cabin block seems a true Civil War pattern, first appearing in the 1860s, perhaps linked to Lincoln's log cabin campaign theme. We can use it to remember Harriet Beecher Stowe's influential book *Uncle Tom's Cabin*, which laid a path toward a war to free the slaves.

Initially published as a newspaper serial in 1851, the story mesmerized readers with a glimpse of life in slavery. Among the readers were Amasa and Sophia Soule's family. Daughter Annie recalled the series years later:

> *"As the drama of* Uncle Tom's Cabin *unrolled in its pages the family would gather in the parlor each Sunday afternoon, and mother would read that week's installment aloud.… What a sensation that story made! No one today can even imagine it. At first mother started to read*

*it to us on Sunday afternoon, so father could be there to hear, but the paper came on Wednesday, and soon we became too eager for it to wait until Sundays…. It was the reading of* Uncle Tom's Cabin *that really made my father hate slavery so bitterly. I can see father yet, striding up and down the room, his hands clenched in fury."*

Published as a book, *Uncle Tom's Cabin* sold 300,000 copies in its first year. It was confiscated, banned, and burned in many areas of the South. Book burners' fear of the written word was well justified. Many remembered that the book changed their lives. The Soule family determined to leave Massachusetts for the Kansas Territory, where they could take a stand in the antislavery struggle.

## Cutting

Refer to the blocks for your shading preferences. Decide whether you want an 8″ × 8″ block or a 12″ × 12″ block (12″ × 12″ block measurements are in parentheses). Cut the following:

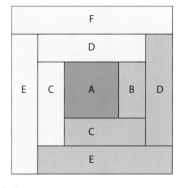

*Note: All the strips (rectangles) are the same width.*

**A:** 1 red square 3⅛″ × 3⅛″ (4½″ × 4½″)

**B:** 1 dark rectangle 1⅞″ × 3⅛″ (2½″ × 4½″)

**C:** 1 light and 1 dark rectangle 1⅞″ × 4½″ (2½″ × 6½″)

**D:** 1 light and 1 dark rectangle 1⅞″ × 5⅞″ (2½″ × 8½″)

**E:** 1 light and 1 dark rectangle 1⅞″ × 7¼″ (2½″ × 10½″)

**F:** 1 light rectangle 1⅞″ × 8⅝″ (2½″ × 12½″)

For a finished 8″ × 8″ block, trim the pieced block to 8½″ × 8½″ (unfinished).

## Reference

Interview with Annie Soule Prentiss, "She Looks Back Seventy-Five Years to the Founding of Lawrence," *Kansas City Star*, January 13, 1929.

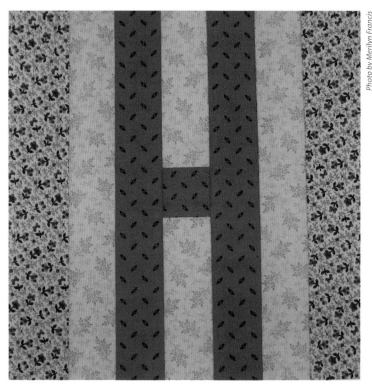

*Photo by Merilyn Francis*

Block by Merilyn Francis

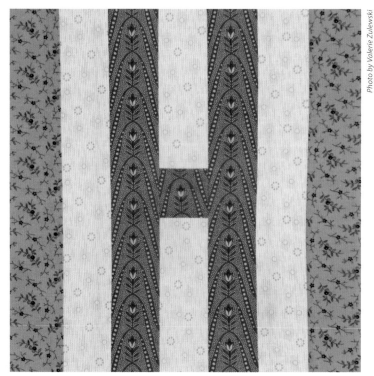

*Photo by Valerie Zulewski*

Block by Valerie Zulewski

The Michigan State Relief Association at a Virginia field hospital. Is that a quilt airing out on the tent?

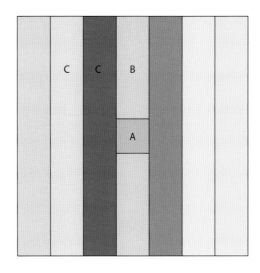

Flags communicate basic information to armies opposed on a battlefield: White banners indicate the familiar signal of surrender. Yellow flags indicated a hospital's no-fire zone. Confederate nurse Kate Cumming explained their use in Corinth, Mississippi:

> "We are at the Tishomingo Hotel, which, like every other large building, has been taken for a hospital. The yellow flag is flying from the top of each. Mrs. Ogden tried to prepare me for the scenes which I should witness upon entering the wards. But alas! Nothing that I had ever heard or read had given me the faintest idea of the horrors witnessed here. I do not think that words are in our vocabulary expressive enough to present to the mind the realities of that sad scene. Certainly, none of the glories of the war were presented here."

Later in the war the Union Army modified the simple yellow rectangle by adding a green H to alert friend and foe that patients were sheltered below it. We can remember the field hospitals with this block, drawn from an antique crib quilt pictured in my book *Civil War Women*. I have no evidence that this pattern, a combination of Log Cabin and Log Fence, held any symbolic meaning, but you can color it in symbolic fashion.

## Cutting

Refer to the blocks for your shading preferences. Decide whether you want an 8″ × 8″ block or a 12″ × 12″ block (12″ × 12″ block measurements are in parentheses). Cut the following:

**A:** 1 green square 1⅝″ × 1⅝″ (2¼″ × 2¼″)

**B:** 2 background yellow prints into rectangles 1⅝″ × 4″ (2¼″ × 5⅝″)

**C:** 2 green and 4 yellow prints into rectangles 1⅝″ × 8½″ (2¼″ × 12½″)

### Hints for piecing

■ *Use a scant ¼″ seam allowance when joining the rectangles for the 8″ × 8″ block.*

■ *For an 8″ × 8″ finished block, trim the pieced block to 8½″ × 8½″ (unfinished). For a 12″ × 12″ finished block, trim the pieced block to 12½″ × 12½″ (unfinished).*

### Reference

*Richard Barksdale Harwell, Kate: The Journal of a Confederate Nurse (Baton Rouge: Louisiana State University Press, 1998), p. 14.*

Block by Becky Brown

Block by Mary Crowther

Making Clothes for the Boys in the Army, detail of Adalbert John Volck's drawing of Confederate women

*Courtesy of the Library of Congress*

Empty Spools reminds us of the war's first months, when women set aside their sewing to cut up textiles for lint and bandages. Sallie Brock Putnam, living at her parents' home in Virginia, was advised by brothers, doctors in the Confederate Army, to organize friends to provide medical supplies including bandages, clothing, bedding, and lint.

> *"Our women for a time suspended the busy operations of the needle … to apply themselves more industriously to the preparation of lint, the rolling of bandages, and the many other nameless necessaries.… No longer the sempstress, every woman of Richmond began to prepare herself for the more difficult and responsible duties of the nurse."*

Doctors believed packing a wound with lint scraped from cotton or linen (actually more raveled than scraped) was an effective treatment method, although our contemporary ideas about infection frown upon packing thread into an open wound. *Peterson's Magazine* advised volunteers to make lint

"of unraveled linen, new or old (the latter preferred). [Cut] it in pieces of four or five inches square."

Northerner Mary Livermore remembered the "lint and bandage" mania.

> *"For a time it was the all absorbing topic.… 'What is the best material for lint?' 'How is it best scraped and prepared?'… Every household gave its leisure time to scraping lint and rolling bandages, till the mighty accumulations compelled the ordering of a halt."*

The block is a variation of one published as Spools by the Ladies' Art Company about 1900. Today we call it Empty Spools, perfect to recall the time when women abandoned sewing baskets to scrape lint.

## Cutting

Refer to the blocks for your shading preferences. Decide whether you want an 8″ × 8″ block or a 12″ × 12″ block (12″ × 12″ block measurements are in parentheses). Cut the following:

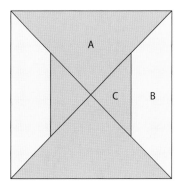

**A:** 1 dark square 9¼″ × 9¼″ (13¼″ × 13¼″) for the spool. Cut in half diagonally twice, creating 4 dark triangles. Discard 2 triangles.

**B:** 2 light rectangles 2½″ × 9¼″ (3½″ × 13¼″). Cut pieces at 45° angles off the edges (see the block) and discard the cut pieces.

**C:** 1 dark square 5¼″ × 5¼″ (7¼″ × 7¼″) for the spool. Cut in half diagonally twice, creating 4 dark triangles. Discard 2 triangles.

### References

Sallie A. Brock, Richmond during the War: Four Years of Personal Observation (New York: G. W. Carleton & Company, 1867), pp. 58 and 59.

Mary A. Livermore, My Story of the War (Hartford: A. D. Worthington, 1889), p. 121.

*Photo by Roseanne Smith*

Block by Roseanne Smith

Block by Barbara Brackman

Winnie Davis behind her mother, Varina Howell Davis; in a print from 1890

Pattern writer Clara Stone named the block Old Maid's Puzzle about 1910. The block can remind us of the women who lived beyond society's definition of women's proper roles, whether by choice or by chance.

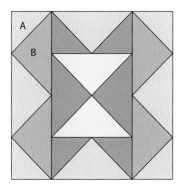

## Cutting

Refer to the blocks for your shading preferences. Decide whether you want an 8″ × 8″ block or a 12″ × 12″ block (12″ × 12″ block measurements are in parentheses). Cut the following:

**A:** 2 medium and 2 dark squares 2⅞″ × 2⅞″ (3⅞″ × 3⅞″). Cut each in half diagonally, creating 4 medium and 4 dark triangles.

**B:** 1 light, 1 medium, 1 medium dark, and 1 dark square 5¼″ × 5¼″ (7¼″ × 7¼″). Cut each in half diagonally twice, creating 4 light, 4 medium, 4 medium dark, and 4 dark triangles. Discard 2 light and 2 dark triangles.

The loss of more than half a million men cost many women any chance of marriage. One of the "old maids" was Jefferson Davis's youngest daughter, Varina Anne, known as Winnie. Born in 1864, she was hailed as the "Daughter of the Confederacy."

In the 1880s Winnie fell in love with Alfred Wilkinson, completely unsuitable in Confederate orthodoxy. Not only a New Yorker with a mother who was Louisa May Alcott's first cousin, he was also grandson to abolitionist Samuel J. May. After five controversial years of engagement, Winnie and Fred broke it off and never saw each other again. Neither ever married.

Was the rift due to finances, Winnie's devotion to her father's memory, or the pressure of a romance played out in newspaper headlines and editorials? We decry celebrity obsession as a peculiarity of the modern age, but these lines from the *New York Times* in 1890 indicate that nothing's new:

## Reference

*Joan E. Cashin, First Lady of the Confederacy: Varina Davis's Civil War (Boston: Harvard University Press, 2008).*

Block by Roseanne Smith

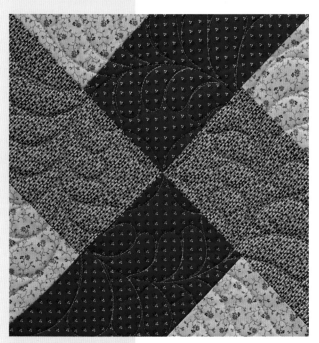

Block by Barbara Brackman

The Twin Sisters: Liberty and Union, a patriotic image used here to sell tobacco

Twin Sisters can stand for the Union and the Confederacy, family locked in a heartbreaking quarrel. None personified the split better than the Todds of Lexington, Kentucky. Mary Todd Lincoln was the Union's First Lady; her half-sister Emilie Todd Helm was married to Confederate General Ben Hardin Helm.

After Ben's death at Chickamauga, Emilie arrived at the White House to stay with her half-sister and brother-in-law. Gossips talked, the press complained, and Lincoln's enemies gloated, but the sisters, dogged by tragedy, consoled each other. Emilie wrote that they could not "open our hearts to each other as freely as we would like. This frightful war comes between us like a barrier of granite closing our lips but not our hearts."

The block was given the name Twin Sisters by the Ladies' Art Company about 1900.

## Cutting

Refer to the blocks for your shading preferences. Decide whether you want an 8″ × 8″ block or a 12″ × 12″ block (12″ × 12″ block measurements are in parentheses). Cut the following:

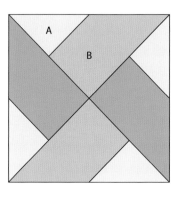

**A:** 1 light square 5¼″ × 5¼″ (7¼″ × 7¼″). Cut in half diagonally twice, creating 4 light triangles.

**B:** 2 medium and 2 dark rectangles 3⅜″ × 6½″ (4¾″ × 9⅜″). Cut a 45° angle off the edges as shown.

Trim and square up the block to size.

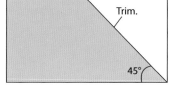

## Reference

*Stephen Berry, House of Abraham: Lincoln and the Todds, a Family Divided by War (Boston: Houghton Mifflin Company, 2007), p. 152.*

Lincoln's casket traveled in a funeral train through seven states, from the capital up to Buffalo, New York, and home to Springfield, Illinois.

Block by Ginny Poplawski

Union Square in New York City was given that name because the spot was at the union of Broadway and the Bowery Road, but the park became the center of many public gatherings during the Civil War: from early rallies and troop reviews to ladies' fund-raising fairs, and finally to Lincoln's funeral after his assassination.

For twenty days in 1865, Americans waited by train tracks to view the president's coffin as it passed. In New York City the procession along Fifth Avenue stopped for orations at the square. One of the 75,000 spectators was six-year-old Theodore Roosevelt, who watched from the second story of his grandfather's house.

The pattern Union Square was given that name in a 1930s Nancy Cabot column in the *Chicago Tribune*.

Block by Ann Champion

## Cutting

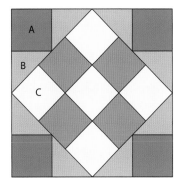

Refer to the blocks for your shading preferences. Decide whether you want an 8″ × 8″ block or a 12″ × 12″ block (12″ × 12″ block measurements are in parentheses). Cut the following:

**A:** 4 dark squares 2½″ × 2½″ (3½″ × 3½″)

**B:** 4 medium squares 2⅞″ × 2⅞″ (3⅞″ × 3⅞″). Cut each in half diagonally, creating 8 medium triangles.

**C:** 5 light and 4 dark squares 2⅜″ × 2⅜″ (3⅜″ × 3⅜″)

*Photo by Roseanne Smith*

Block by Roseanne Smith

Block by Barbara Brackman

Timothy O'Sullivan photographed the McLeans on the back porch of their newly historical home after the surrender at Appomattox. Virginia McLean sits on the porch to the right of her husband, with daughters and a grandchild below. She was in her late 40s at the time. Wilmer had turned 50.

Wilmer McLean liked to say that the Civil War began and ended at his house. He had a point. With his wife, Virginia Hooe McLean, he lived near the Manassas battlefield. In the summer of 1861, a cannonball from that first big battle crashed into the chimney and fell into a simmering pot of stew.

The McLeans moved to a quieter part of Virginia near a small town called Appomattox Court House. In April 1865, negotiators working on surrender terms persuaded Mr. McLean to offer the parlor of his substantial brick home for the signing of the terms. The parlor was handsome and the furniture fashionable, a dignified room in which to end a horrible war.

Virginia McLean's Appomattox parlor suffered more damage than her kitchen near Manassas. Souvenir collectors immediately stripped the room, carrying away the chairs that Generals Lee and Grant had sat upon and the tables that had held the papers. Virginia McLean's trials were minor in the larger context of Civil War, but like so many Southern women who had been rich before the war, she spent the rest of her life with only memories of prosperity. Two years after Appomattox, the McLeans lost their brick house because they could not pay the mortgage.

Courthouse Square recalls the surrender agreed upon in that parlor in Appomattox Court House. The block dates to the 1840s, the days of the album quilt fashion, a variation of a pattern given that name by Carrie Hall in her 1935 book *Romance of the Patchwork Quilt*.

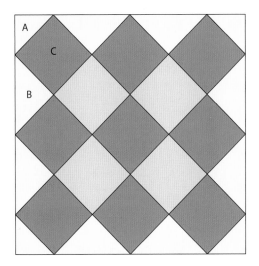

## Cutting

Refer to the blocks for your shading preferences. Decide whether you want an 8″ × 8″ block or a 12″ × 12″ block (12″ × 12″ block measurements are in parentheses). Cut the following:

**A:** 2 light squares 2¼″ × 2¼″ (2⅞″ × 2⅞″). Cut each in half diagonally, creating 4 light triangles.

**B:** 2 light squares 3⅞″ × 3⅞″ (5¼″ × 5¼″). Cut each in half diagonally twice, creating 8 light triangles.

**C:** 4 light and 9 dark squares 2⅜″ × 2⅜″ (3⅜″ × 3⅜″)

Trim and square up the block to size.

## Reference

*Geoffrey C. Ward, Ken Burns, and Ric Burns, The Civil War: An Illustrated History (New York: Random House, 1992), p. xix.*

*Photo by Becky Brown*

Block by Becky Brown

*Photo by Kathie Coombs*

Block by Kathie Coombs

Faces of slavery in a photograph by James F. Gibson, taken at a plantation in Pamunkey Run, Virginia, 1862. That's a shaggy dog in the foreground.

Right Hand of Friendship reminds us that an Underground Railroad continued during the war. In 1863 Archer Alexander, living in slavery near St. Louis, heard of a planned bridge attack by Southern guerillas and ran to a Union neighbor's home with a warning. When he realized the punishment that spying would earn him, he kept running into the city, where he met William Greenleaf Eliot, a Unitarian minister with abolitionist sympathies. Eliot agreed to hire Archer and offered to buy his freedom and that of his wife, Louisa, who was left at home with no idea of Archer's whereabouts.

Louisa received a letter with the offer but dictated a sad reply:

> "[I] lost no time in asking Mr. Jim if he would sell me, and what he would take for me. He flew at me, and said I would never get free only at the point of the Baynot [bayonet], and there was no use in my ever speaking to him any more about it.… He is watching me night and day.… I had good courage all along until now, but now I am almost heart-broken."

Despite Mr. Jim's vigilance, Louisa and a daughter escaped, carried to the city by a neighbor who agreed for a $20 fee to hide her in the oxcart he drove to the city market. Louisa and Archer couldn't read or write, yet they managed to hatch a complex plan by mail. We tend to think that illiterate people were deprived of written communication (a possible reason for tales of secret visual codes), but many social systems helped those who couldn't write. Sympathetic neighbors took Louisa's dictation and delivered her mail—an informal and illegal post office.

The quilt block Right Hand of Friendship was published by *Hearth & Home* magazine in the early twentieth century.

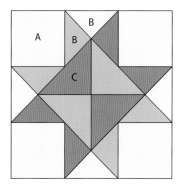

## Cutting

Refer to the blocks for your shading preferences. Decide whether you want an 8″ × 8″ block or a 12″ × 12″ block (12″ × 12″ block measurements are in parentheses). Cut the following:

**A:** 4 light squares 3⅛″ × 3⅛″ (4½″ × 4½″)

**B:** 1 light, 1 medium, and 1 dark square 3⅞″ × 3⅞″ (5¼″ × 5¼″). Cut each in half diagonally twice, creating 4 light, 4 medium, and 4 dark triangles.

**C:** 1 medium and 1 dark square 3½″ × 3½″ (4⅞″ × 4⅞″). Cut each in half diagonally, creating 2 medium and 2 dark triangles.

## Reference

*William Greenleaf Eliot, The Story of Archer Alexander: From Slavery to Freedom (Boston: Cupples, Upham, 1885).*

Block by Quilt4Fun

Block by Molly Mandeville Fryer

Mary Chesnut watched the battle from the roof of her Charleston house, a scene pictured in *Harper's Weekly*, May 4, 1861.

The Fort Sumter block recalls the official beginning of the Civil War with the Confederate bombardment of the Union fort in Charleston's harbor. Southern diarist Mary Chesnut was a witness as her husband negotiated with the Yankees on the island.

> "I do not pretend to go to sleep. How can I? If [the Union commander] does not accept terms at four, the orders are, he shall be fired upon. I count four, St. Michael's bells chime out and I begin to hope. At half past four, the heavy booming of a cannon. I sprang out of bed, and on my knees prostrate I prayed as I never prayed before.

> "There was a sound of stir all over the house, pattering of feet in the corridors. All seemed hurrying one way. I put on my double gown and a shawl and went, too. It was to the housetop. The shells were bursting. In the dark I heard a man say, 'Waste of ammunition.' I knew my husband was rowing about in a boat somewhere in that dark bay, and that the shells were roofing it over, bursting toward the fort."

The block, named by the fictional Nancy Cabot, who wrote a quilt column for the *Chicago Tribune* in the 1930s, seems to symbolize the fort in the harbor. The central nine-patch can stand for the building, the blue triangles around it symbolize the harbor, and the corner shapes in red represent the cannon fire from the shore.

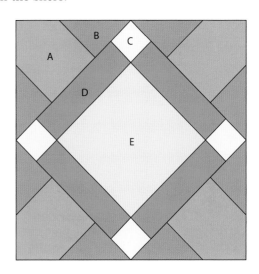

## Cutting

Refer to the blocks for your shading preferences. Decide whether you want an 8″ × 8″ block or a 12″ × 12″ block (12″ × 12″ block measurements are in parentheses). Cut the following:

**A:** 4 red rectangles 2½″ × 3½″ (3⅜″ × 5″). You'll trim the outside points at 90° angles when you've finished piecing the block, and square up the block to the correct size.

**B:** 2 blue squares 3⅞″ × 3⅞″ (5¼″ × 5¼″). Cut each in half diagonally twice, creating 8 blue triangles.

**C:** 4 light squares 1½″ × 1½″ (1⅞″ × 1⅞″)

**D:** 4 dark rectangles 1½″ × 4⅛″ (1⅞″ × 6¼″)

**E:** 1 medium square 4⅛″ × 4⅛″ (6¼″ × 6¼″)

## Reference

*C. Vann Woodward (editor), Mary Chesnut's Civil War (New Haven: Yale University Press, 1993), p. 46.*

Block by Becky Brown

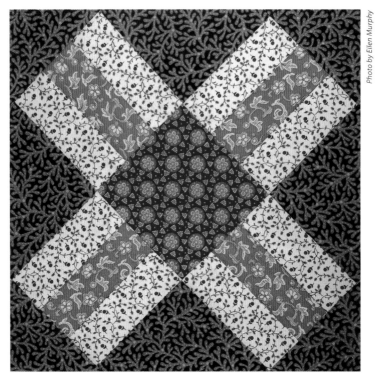

*Photo by Ellen Murphy*

Block by Ellen Murphy from American Homestead

On the way to Manassas, Union troops leaving Washington

At the beginning of the war that was supposed to last only a few months, Confederate recruits gathered in Virginia at the crossing of two railroads, the Manassas Gap and the Orange and Alexandria. Union troops planned to march through the junction on their glorious path to Confederate Richmond. Excited Washingtonians followed the federal army, carrying picnic baskets for a summer outing while witnessing Union troops put short end to the war.

A correspondent for the *Boston Transcript* described the morning when the army began their march toward the "land o' Dixie":

> *"The sun shone brilliantly, and the fresh morning air was highly invigorating. The troops on foot started off as joyfully as if they were bound upon a New England picnic, or a clambake; and not the slightest exhibition of fear or uneasiness, even, as to what might possibly be in store for the brave fellows...."*

Untrained Yankee and rebel armies met at a creek named Bull Run, where thousands of Southerners held their ground. Amazed at the number of opposition troops, the federal army fled in chaos, running panicked spectators off the roads back to the Union capital. This Confederate victory jolted North and South into realizing it was not to be a 30-day war.

Railroad Crossing can remember this first major land battle, called by the Confederacy the Battle of Manassas, and by the Union the Battle of Bull Run.

The patchwork pattern Railroad Crossing was given that name in 1935 in the *Kansas City Star*'s quilt column.

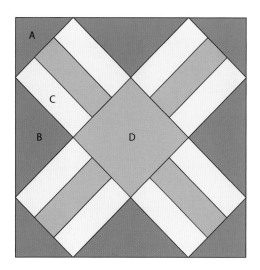

## Cutting

Refer to the blocks for your shading preferences. Decide whether you want an 8″ × 8″ block or a 12″ × 12″ block (12″ × 12″ block measurements are in parentheses). Cut the following:

**A:** 2 dark squares 2⅞″ × 2⅞″ (3⅞″ × 3⅞″). Cut each in half diagonally, creating 4 dark triangles.

**B:** 1 dark square 5¼″ × 5¼″ (7¼″ × 7¼″). Cut in half diagonally twice, creating 4 dark triangles.

**C:** 8 light and 4 medium rectangles 1½″ × 3⅜″ (1⅞″ × 4¾″)

**D:** 1 medium square 3⅜″ × 3⅜″ (4¾″ × 4¾″)

---

### Hints for piecing

- *For the finished 8″ × 8″ block, use a generous ¼″ seam allowance when joining the C rectangles.*

- *For the finished 12″ × 12″ block, use a scant ¼″ seam allowance when joining the C rectangles.*

---

**Reference**
G.P.R., "Letter," Boston Transcript, July 16, 1861.

*Photo by Sue Flego*

Block by Sue Flego

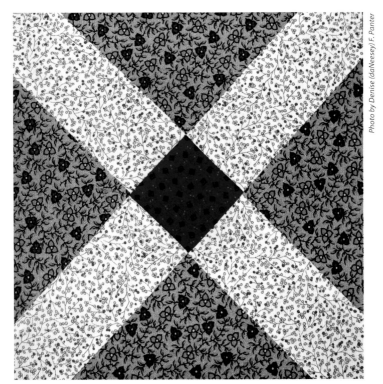

*Photo by Denise (daNeesey) F. Panter*

Block by Denise (daNeesey) F. Panter

Barges on the Ohio River, from *Harper's Weekly*

When rivers were the nation's transportation cross-roads, the junction of the Ohio and Mississippi Rivers in western Kentucky was at the heart of the conflict. Kentucky, a slave state with split loyalties, began the war as officially neutral, but neutrality was impossible to maintain. Union sympathizers gained political strength in 1861, so Confederate troops marched in to secure the all-important Mississippi, claiming the town of Columbus, Kentucky, and the river below it. Yankees parried by sending General Ulysses S. Grant's Union army to occupy Paducah, Kentucky, at the junction of the Ohio and Tennessee Rivers, ensuring that the North controlled the Ohio River. Paducah remained under Union occupation for the duration of the war, and Kentucky remained a Union state.

*Harper's Weekly* sketched Paducah shortly after the Union army took over:

> *"… a beautiful little city, full of respectable and often elegant residences. It now wears, however, a deserted and melancholy appearance. Whole streets of tenantless buildings stretch from the landing to the intrenchments; and the few inhabitants who remain, although entirely unmolested and secure, look guilty and sullen.*

> *"Some of our boys left the steamer Sunday, and, wandering about the town, took possession of the deserted choir of a Secesh [secessionist] church, and one of our number being a good organist, and most of us having assisted before on such occasions, we did our best to convince those within hearing that, although belonging to the 'Northern rabble,' we were not altogether heathen and benighted."*

The pattern, better known as an album block, was given the name Kentucky Crossroads in an early-twentieth-century magazine. My source is a clipping in an old scrapbook.

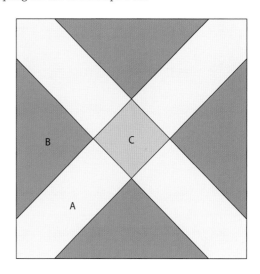

## Cutting

Refer to the blocks for your shading preferences. Decide whether you want an 8″ × 8″ block or a 12″ × 12″ block (12″ × 12″ block measurements are in parentheses). Cut the following:

**A:** 4 light rectangles 2⅜″ × 5½″ (3⅜″ × 7⅞″). You'll trim these at the end.

**B:** 1 dark square 6⅝″ × 6⅝″ (9¼″ × 9¼″). Cut in half diagonally twice, creating 4 dark triangles.

**C:** 1 medium square 2⅜″ × 2⅜″ (3⅜″ × 3⅜″)

Trim and square up the block.

## Reference

J.C. Beard, "Our Paducah Sketches," *Harper's Weekly*, October 26, 1861.

*Photo by Ann Champion*

Block by Ann Champion

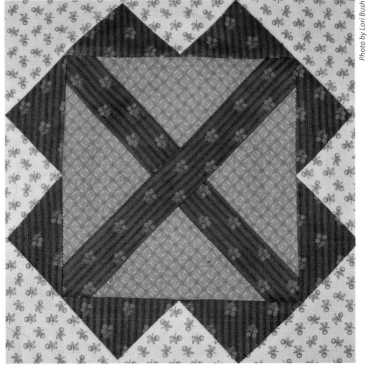

*Photo by Lori Bush*

Block by Debbie Gilsdorf

Sam Houston in 1858

Texas Tears seems a good way to recall Sam Houston and the war in Texas. The block is a variation of one printed about 1890 by the Ladies' Art Company.

## Cutting

Refer to the blocks for your shading preferences. Decide whether you want an 8″ × 8″ block or a 12″ × 12″ block (12″ × 12″ block measurements are in parentheses). Cut the following:

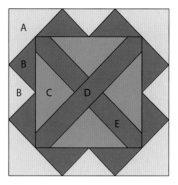

**A:** 2 light squares 3⁹⁄₁₆″ × 3⁹⁄₁₆″ (just under 3⅝″on the ruler*) (4⅞″ × 4⅞″). Cut each in half diagonally, creating 4 light triangles.

**B:** 1 light and 2 dark squares 3¹⁵⁄₁₆″ × 3¹⁵⁄₁₆″ (just under 4″ on the ruler*) (5¼″ × 5¼″). Cut each in half diagonally twice, creating 4 light and 8 dark triangles.

**C:** 1 medium square 5¼″ × 5¼″ (7⅛″ × 7⅛″). Cut in half diagonally twice, creating 4 medium triangles.

**D:** 1 dark rectangle 1⁷⁄₁₆″ × 8¾″ (2″ × 12¼″)

**E:** 2 dark rectangles 1⁷⁄₁₆″ × 4¼″ (2″ × 5¾″)

*A ¹⁄₁₆″ is in the middle of the ⅛″ increments on the ruler.

---

*Hints for piecing*

■ *For the finished 8″ × 8″ block, trim the center square to 5⅞″ × 5⅞″. For the finished 12″ x 12″ block, trim to 8½″ × 8½″.*

■ *For best results, use a color scheme similar to that of the pictured blocks.*

---

The Civil War put an end to Sam Houston's political career. Almost 70 when it began, he'd been governor of both Tennessee and Texas, president of the Texas Republic, and a senator from the state. The proud and independent Houston defined the mythical Texan. He was known for wearing a broad-brimmed hat at a time when top hats were the fashion, and he wore a vest of wildcat fur and a Mexican serape as an overcoat.

Houston was a slave owner but opposed the idea that states could secede, a threat that so-called fire-eaters had been using to hold the federal government political hostage for decades. As threats grew louder, Houston successfully ran for Texas governor on a Union platform. When the fire-eaters played their secession card in 1861, he refused to permit Texas to join the Confederacy and was forced out of office.

President Lincoln asked Houston to lead Union troops against a Confederate Texas, but he rejected that offer. Opposed to a war he knew the South couldn't win, he also refused to wear the Confederate uniform. Houston was a Southern politician with a realistic vision of the costs of war, a man who acted according to his conscience rather than the public consensus.

## Reference

*James L. Haley, Sam Houston (Norman: University of Oklahoma Press, 2004).*

*Photo by Becky Brown*

Block by Becky Brown

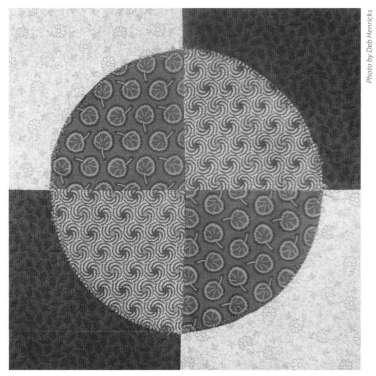

*Photo by Deb Henricks*

Block by Deb Henricks

*Harper's Weekly* suggested that female traitors be sentenced to wear unfashionable clothing.

poisonous snakes in the grass. But the Copperheads took the label for a compliment, as copper pennies of the day featured the Liberty head. Many wore Liberty-head copper pennies as jewelry to show their loyalty to the Peace Democrat cause.

We tend to look back at the war as cut and dried, North and South, puzzling at gray shadings of political position. To remember the Indiana secessionists, we can stitch an old design, Indiana Puzzle, given that name by pattern designer Carlie Sexton in the 1920s. Make it up in copper-colored prints and it will be particularly appropriate, representing the copper penny worn by some to flaunt their stand against the war.

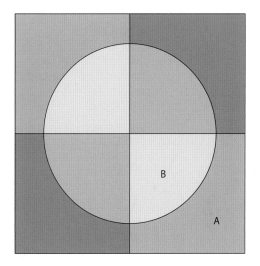

Indiana Puzzle recalls politics in that Union state, where a number of men and women expressed opposition to the war, a hatred of Lincoln, and a desire to secede. Mary Kemper Vermilion was from a family of abolitionists, strong believers in the Union cause. When her husband went off to fight, he left her with his parents in Indiana. She found the neighbors' ideas upsetting.

> "Indiana, they say, is on the verge of revolution. Day before yesterday they had wild times at Indianapolis. The secesh tried to get possession of the arsenal, but were prevented by the Governor who called out the militia…. The democrats … don't propose yet to join Jeff Davis's Confederacy, but to form a Southwestern confederacy of their own."

These Democrats opposed to the war favored an immediate truce with the Confederacy. Mary and her fellow Republicans called them Copperheads,

## Cutting

Refer to the blocks for your shading preferences. Decide whether you want an 8″ × 8″ block or a 12″ × 12″ block. Cut the following:

**A:** 2 medium and 2 dark shapes A using the pattern (page 101)

**B:** 2 light and 2 medium light quarter-circles using the pattern (page 101)

## Reference

*Donald C. Elder III (editor), Love amid the Turmoil: The Civil War Letters of William and Mary Vermilion (Iowa City: The University of Iowa Press, 2003), p. 44.*

*Photo by Jo Schreiber*

Block by Jo Schreiber

*Photo by Lorraine Heley*

Block by Lorraine Heley

Courtesy of the Library of Congress

Julia Ward Howe, engraving by Caroline Amelia Powell after an earlier photo by Josiah Hawes

Julia Ward Howe's biography tells how she composed "Battle Hymn of the Republic."

*"Returning from a review of troops … she and her companions sang, to beguile the tedium of the way, the war songs which everyone was singing in those days; among them—'John Brown's body lies a mouldering in the grave. His soul is marching on!'*

*"The soldiers liked this, cried, 'Good for you!' and took up the chorus with its rhythmic swing. 'Mrs. Howe,' said [her companion], 'Why do you not write some good words for that stirring tune?'"*

Inspired that night, she awoke to imagine words:

*"Line by line, stanza by stanza … She waited till the voice was silent, till the last line was ended; then sprang from bed, and groping for pen and paper, scrawled in the gray twilight the 'Battle Hymn of the Republic.'"*

The poem published in the *Atlantic Monthly* became "the word of the hour." Her song still has a strong hold upon Americans.

*Mine eyes have seen the glory of the coming of the Lord:*

*He is trampling out the vintage where the grapes of wrath are stored;*

*He hath loosed the fateful lightning of His terrible swift sword:*

*His truth is marching on.*

Her phrases drawn from her knowledge of the Bible have become English icons. The "grapes of wrath" comes from the Book of Revelation—fruit pressed into "the great winepress of the wrath of God." The block here is a variation of a traditional pattern called Grape Basket by the Ladies' Art Company in the late nineteenth century. Similar blocks date to the Civil War.

## Cutting

Refer to the blocks for your shading preferences. Decide whether you want an 8″ × 8″ block or a 12″ × 12″ block (12″ × 12″ block measurements are in parentheses). Cut the following:

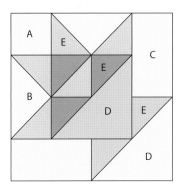

**A:** 1 light square 2½″ × 2½″ (3½″ × 3½″)

**B:** 1 light square 5¼″ × 5¼″ (7¼″ × 7¼″). Cut in half diagonally twice, creating 4 light triangles. Discard 2 triangles.

**C:** 2 light rectangles 2½″ × 4½″ (3½″ × 6½″)

**D:** 1 light square and 1 gold square 4⅞″ × 4⅞″ (6⅞″ × 6⅞″). Cut each in half diagonally, creating 2 light and 2 gold triangles. Discard 1 light and 1 gold triangle.

**E:** 3 light purple, 2 dark purple, and 1 gold square 2⅞″ × 2⅞″ (3⅞″ × 3⅞″). Cut each in half diagonally, creating 6 light purple, 4 dark purple, and 2 gold triangles. Discard 1 light purple and 1 dark purple triangle.

## Reference

*Laura E. Richards and Maud Howe Elliott, Julia Ward Howe, 1819–1910 (Boston, New York: Houghton Mifflin Company, 1915), p. 187.*

Block by Becky Brown

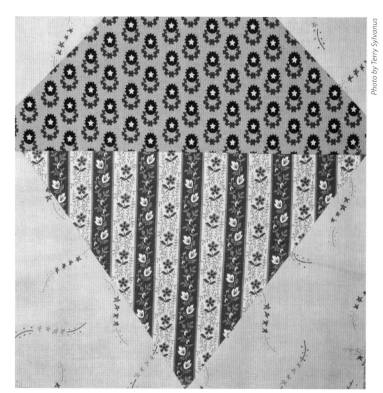

Block by Terry Sylvanus

*Courtesy of the Library of Congress*

Image from a patriotic Union envelope

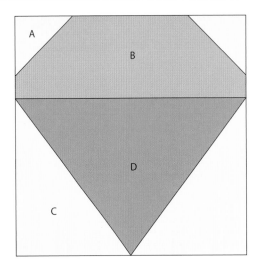

The United States has been viewed as the "Shield of Liberty" since Revolutionary times. When devising symbolism for the new republic, the Founding Fathers drafted an eagle with a shield on its breast. Various arrangements of stars and stripes were proposed. The final version of the shield works so well it is hard to imagine that other designs were considered.

We see shields in American quilts from the beginning of the nineteenth century, but the early versions were generally carried by the eagle. A lone shield became a favorite design for appliqué artists during the Civil War and into the 1870s. Here we have a new shield block, pieced from striped and starry fabrics.

## Cutting

Refer to the blocks for your shading preferences. Decide whether you want an 8″ × 8″ block or a 12″ × 12″ block (12″ × 12″ block measurements are in parentheses). Cut the following:

**A:** 1 light square 2⅞″ × 2⅞″ (3⅞″ × 3⅞″). Cut in half diagonally, creating 2 light triangles.

**B:** 1 starry blue rectangle 3¼″ × 8½″ (4⅝″ × 12½″). Trim using pattern B (page 102 or 103).

**C:** 2 light rectangles 4¾″ × 6¼″ (6¾″ × 8⅞″). Place the rectangles right sides together and cut diagonally from corner to corner to make 4 triangles. Discard 2.

**D:** Cut a striped red fabric into a rectangle 9″ × 5⅞″ (13″ × 8½″). The stripes should run vertically. Trim using pattern D (page 102 or 103) into a triangle.

If you are a new piecer, you might want to save these blocks untill the end of your sampler. Each requires set-in seams (Y-seams) that can be a little tricky at first.

Block by Merilyn Francis

Block by Anne Brill

Martinsburg changed flags more than 30 times during the war. This picture from *Harper's Weekly* shows the town under a Confederate flag in 1861.

West Virginia recalls a state created when part of Virginia seceded from the Confederacy. Many Virginians in the state's mountainous northwest believed their interests lay with the Union and proposed a state of Kanawha, named after the river that flows through the region. Kanawha was rejected, as were suggestions Allegheny, Columbia, and New Virginia. The state of West Virginia became the 35th star on the Union flag.

West Virginia's hills continued as a battleground as armies occupied and retreated. Sixteen-year-old Sirene Bunten wrote about Southern soldiers who came to dinner and tried to persuade her to abandon her Unionist views. The family managed to keep their cows but lost some bedding.

*"There was eleven rebels ate supper here last night. There was one Lieut. here and he kept his men straight…. That Lieut. tried very hard to make Harry and I rebels but he had to give it up. They camped down at E.G. Burr's last night. Late. There was about six hundred rebels passed here today, they were driving cattle and I just expected they would take ours but they did not. They took Chet's but the girls got them back. It was a curious body of soldiers, they were dressed in all colors. They robbed the stores and houses all along the road. They took one blanket from us."*

West Virginia is a variation of a pattern published about 1915 by *Hearth & Home* magazine when the editors asked readers for a block for each state.

## Cutting

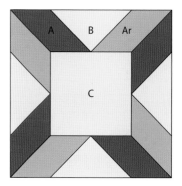

Refer to the blocks for your shading preferences. Decide whether you want an 8″ × 8″ block or a 12″ × 12″ block (12″ × 12″ block measurements are in parentheses). Cut the following:

**A:** 4 red and 4 blue rectangles 1⅞″ × 5⅜″ (2⅝″ × 7¼″). Cut 4 parallelograms of each color by trimming a 45° angle off each inside end (near the block center) as shown. All the red shapes go one way and all the blues are reversed. Remember that these are not diamonds with 4 equal sides, but they are longer on 2 sides.

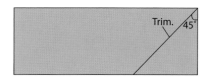

**B:** 1 light square 5¼″ × 5¼″ (7¼″ × 7¼″). Cut in half diagonally twice, creating 4 light triangles.

**C:** 1 light square 4½″ × 4½″ (6½″ × 6½″)

### Reference

*Excerpts from Sirene Bunten's diary, www.wvculture.org > Search "Sirene Bunten." Accessed July 2011.*

Block by Becky Brown

Charleston, the heart of the Confederacy, suffered badly. George N. Barnard's 1865 photo shows a man sitting in the ruins of Secession Hall.

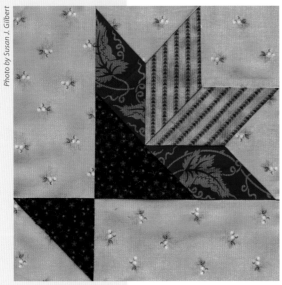

Block by Susan J. Gilbert

Emma Holmes was 23 when the war began, one of eleven children of a widow in Charleston, South Carolina. She recorded the meetings of various aid societies in her diary.

> *"This afternoon the Ladies Charleston Volunteer Aid Society held a meeting at the S.C. Hall. 192 ladies were there and nearly $1000 collected from subscriptions and donations.… 12 Managers [will] cut out the work and distribute it. The ladies all seemed to enjoy seeing their friends as well as the purpose for which they came."*

A few months later, Emma recorded a report from the Ladies' Society for Clothing the Troops in Active Service: "2301 flannel shirts and drawers have been completed, two or three companies going on have been supplied, and the rest sent to the quarter-master."

Friends visited Emma's home to make socks and slippers.

> *"Out of the eleven ladies gathered, eight were knitting stockings, and grandmother showed us a pair of slippers sent her from London just after she was married, when it was the fashion for the ladies to make their own for drawing room wear."*

The block to recall Carolina's needlework organizations is a variation of what today's quilters would call a Carolina Lily, published in 1909 by the *Ladies' Home Journal* as Flower Pot. The single bloom can symbolize the botanical Carolina lily (*Lilium michauxii*), a wildflower similar to the tiger lily that grows throughout the Carolinas.

# Cutting

Refer to the blocks for your shading preferences. Decide whether you want an 8″ × 8″ block or a 12″ × 12″ block (12″ × 12″ block measurements are in parentheses). Cut the following:

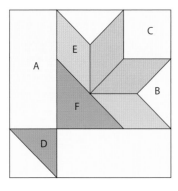

**A:** 2 light rectangles 2⅞″ × 6⅛″ (4″ × 9″)

**B:** 1 light square 4½″ × 4½″ (6¼″ × 6¼″). Cut in half diagonally twice, creating 4 light triangles. Discard 2 light triangles.

**C:** 1 light square 2⅞″ × 2⅞″ (4″ × 4″)

**D:** 1 light and 1 dark green square 3¼″ × 3¼″ (4⅜″ × 4⅜″). Cut each in half diagonally, creating 2 light and 2 dark triangles. Discard 1 triangle of each color.

**E:** 2 gold and 2 light green rectangles 2⅛″ × 5¼″ (3″ × 7¼″). Trim 45° angles as shown and discard the cut pieces. You can cut the pieces as shown or use the patterns (below).

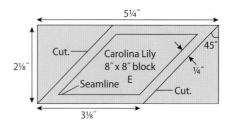

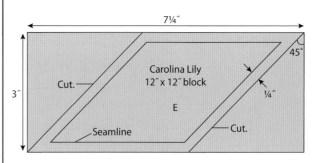

**F:** Cut 1 dark green square 4⅛″ × 4⅛″ (5⅞″ × 5⅞″). Cut in half diagonally, creating 2 dark green triangles. Discard 1 triangle.

## Reference

John F. Marszalek, *The Diary of Miss Emma Holmes, 1861–1866* (Baton Rouge: University of Louisiana Press, 1994).

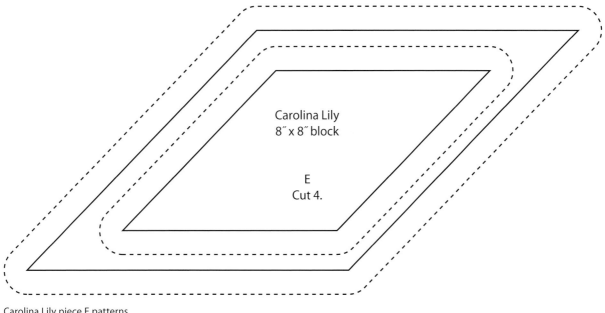

Carolina Lily
8″ x 8″ block

E
Cut 4.

Carolina Lily piece E patterns

Block by Carol Sanderson

Block by Becky Brown

Confederate General Albert Sydney Johnston was killed at the Battle of Shiloh in 1862.

In 1884 newspapers announced the discovery of a rose that changed color during the day. "The 'Confederate rose' is the name of a new flower which is white in the morning and red at night. Four of them have been planted around the grave of Gen. Albert Sydney Johnston in the State cemetery at Austin."

A skeptical editor at the *Gardener's Monthly and Horticulturist* wrote:

> *"We do not know of any rose under this name. There are flowers which open white, and become pinkish when they fade, but we do not know of any rose which does this. It is barely possible that this is an exaggeration of some such fact, though still more possible that it is one of those silly paragraphs of a 'smart' reporter, which do no credit to the newspaper press."*

Ten years later a botanist identified it in *Garden and Forest* as a hibiscus:

> *"Hibiscus mutabilis, Cotton Rose, or Confederate Rose, is a small tree of rather open habit. I first noticed it in the gardens of New Orleans, and later at Mobile, Pensacola and Jacksonville. It is a fine plant when in bloom, bearing at the same time white and red flowers, and thus presenting a very striking appearance."*

The quilt block is based on a Confederate Rose pattern that Nancy Cabot, the quilt columnist at the *Chicago Tribune*, published in the 1930s.

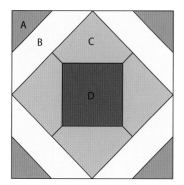

## Cutting

Refer to the blocks for your shading preferences. Decide whether you want an 8″ × 8″ block or a 12″ × 12″ block (12″ × 12″ block measurements are in parentheses). Cut the following:

**A:** 2 dark squares 2⅞″ × 2⅞″ (3⅞″ × 3⅞″). Cut each in half diagonally, creating 4 dark triangles.

**B:** 4 light rectangles 1⅞″ × 6⅞″ (2⅝″ × 9¾″). Trim the corners at 45° angles as shown in the block or use the patterns (page 104).

**C:** 4 medium shapes from the patterns (page 104)

**D:** 1 dark square 3½″ × 3½″ (5″ × 5″)

### References

*The Gardener's Monthly and Horticulturist*, Volume 26, Number 304, April 1884, p. 103.

*Garden & Forest*, Volume 7, February 14, 1894, p. 63.

*Photo by Merilyn Francis*

Block by Merilyn Francis

*Photo by Becky Brown*

Block by Becky Brown

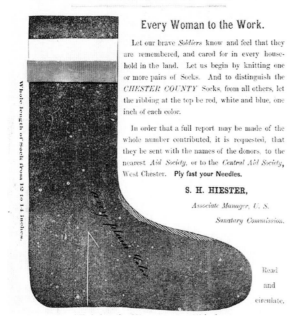

"Ply fast your needles!"—patriotic socks for soldiers

Patriotic Yankees and rebels alike wore the red, white, and blue colors in everything from hat ribbons and suspenders down to hand-knit socks, as knitting needles became the newest ladies' accessory.

Rebel Mary Chesnut wrote in the war's first summer:

> "I do not know when I have seen a woman without knitting in her hand. Socks for the soldiers *is the cry.* One poor man said he had dozens of socks and but one shirt. He preferred more shirts and less stockings. It gives a quaint look, the twinkling of needles, and the everlasting sock dangling."

This patriotic pieced star was published long after the war as a red, white, and blue quilt in the agricultural magazine *Orange Judd Farmer* in 1898.

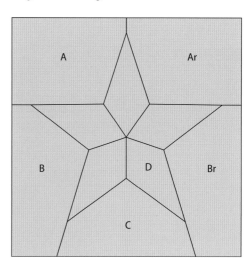

## Cutting

Refer to the blocks for your shading preferences. Decide if you want an 8″ × 8″ block or a 12″ × 12″ block. See the patterns (pages 105–106) and cut as directed.

### Reference

*C. Vann Woodward (editor), Mary Chesnut's Civil War (New Haven: Yale University Press, 1993), p. 167.*

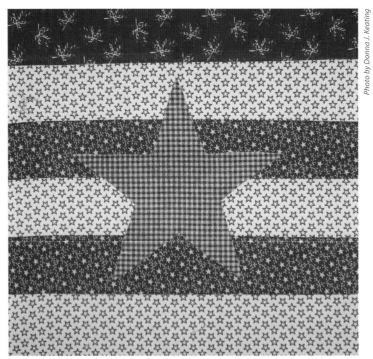

*Photo by Donna J. Keating*

Block by Donna J. Keating aka Quilting Bear Gal

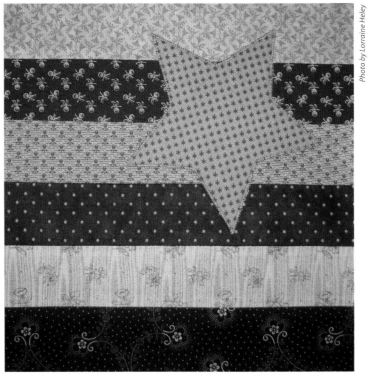

*Photo by Lorraine Heley*

Block by Lorraine Heley

Mary Rockhold Teter made this quilt, pictured in *Peterson's Magazine*. Collection of the Smithsonian Institution.

In July 1861, *Peterson's Magazine* published a color sketch of *The Stars and Stripes Bed Quilt*, the earliest color quilt pattern yet found in an American periodical. The original pattern, inspiring this one, called for 34 stars in a blue field floating on red and white stripes.

*Peterson's* was a women's periodical with fashion, fiction, household advice, craft patterns, and decorating tips. (Things haven't changed much in the women's magazine business.) The publishers used "clubs" to expand their subscription list, encouraging readers to earn a discount and prizes by selling subscriptions to their friends.

Mary Kemper Vermilion, living in Iowa with family while her husband fought for the Union, wrote her husband of all the neighborhood happenings. In one letter, dated December 1, 1863, she wrote,

> *"Mrs. Paschal … is making a club for* Peterson's Magazine *and she came to get me to subscribe. I didn't do it. I told her I didn't care much for ladies magazines while the war lasts, and then there are others that I would much rather have than* Peterson's.…"

Mary was a strong Union supporter who apparently found wartime entertainment frivolous. Or it might be that she preferred *Peterson's* chief rival, *Godey's Lady's Book*.

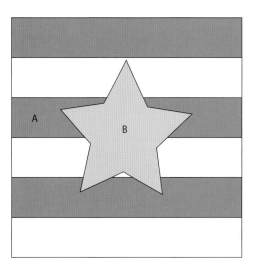

## Cutting

Decide whether you want an 8″ × 8″ block or a 12″ × 12″ block (12″ × 12″ block measurements are in parentheses). Cut the following:

**A:** 3 red and 3 white rectangles 1⅞″ × 8½″ (2½″ × 12½″).

**B:** 1 blue star using the pattern (page 107)*

*Remember to add a seam allowance around each appliqué piece if using a turn-under method of appliqué.*

> ### Hint for piecing
> *Use a generous ¼″ seam allowance when joining the red and white rectangles for the finished 8″ × 8″ block.*

## Reference

Donald C. Elder III (editor), *Love amid the Turmoil: The Civil War Letters of William and Mary Vermilion* (Iowa City: The University of Iowa Press, 2003), pp. 265.

Photo by Becky Brown

Block by Becky Brown

Photo by Leonie Weatherley

Block by Leonie Weatherley

Painter George Caleb Bingham's *Martial Law* dramatized Order No. 11, creating a lasting vision of Union soldiers expelling Missouri civilians.

*and vehicles of every shape and size and of all kinds, drawn by teams of every sort, except good ones; a cloud of dust rising from the road almost the whole day.… On every road that led eastward from the county of Jackson came the moving mass of humanity, seeking an asylum they knew not where.… Women were seen walking the crowded and dusty road, carrying in a little bundle their all, or at least all they could carry."*

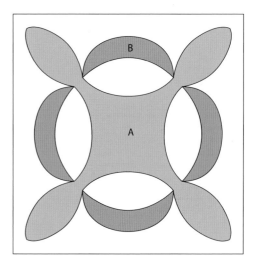

Known also as the Reel or Hickory Leaf, this appliqué pattern dates back to the 1830s. It was given a new name in 1929 when *Kansas City Star* pattern columnist Ruby Short McKim published the story of Order No. 11: "Fannie Kreeger Haller—a 10-year-old girl, saw her mother's choice new quilt snatched from their bed by marauders.… She carried the treasured design in her mind and years after reproduced the quilt christening it Order No. 11.…"

Fannie was one of thousands of western Missourians who never forgot the 1863 Union order to evacuate four counties in the hopes of eliminating Confederate guerillas. Those suspected of Southern sympathies were forced from their homes and lost everything they could not carry.

Union man Martin Rice stayed on his farm and watched the refugees.

*"I saw much of the incidents and the fruits of Order No. 11. Before and behind was seen the long, moving train of sorrowing exiles: wagons*

## Cutting

Refer to the blocks for your shading preferences. Decide whether you want an 8″ × 8″ block or a 12″ × 12″ block (12″ × 12″ block measurements are in parentheses). Cut the following:

1 background square 8½″ × 8½″ (12½″ × 12½″)

**A:** 1 piece A using the pattern (page 108 or 109)*

**B:** 4 of piece B using the pattern (page 108 or 109)*

*Remember to add a seam allowance around each appliqué piece if using a turn-under method of appliqué.*

### References

*Ruby S. McKim, "Order Number 11," Kansas City Star, November 23, 1929.*

*Martin Rice, Rural Rhymes, and Talks and Tales of Olden Times (Kansas City: Hudson Kimberley Publishing Company, 1893), p. 115.*

Block by Quilt4Fun

Block by Valerie Zulewski

The first secessionist flags featured blue fields with an arrangement of seven stars to honor the states that joined the Confederacy in the first months of the war. The Seven Sisters were South Carolina, Mississippi, Florida, Alabama, Georgia, Louisiana, and Texas. After Fort Sumter four more states seceded, and the flag was reworked because the first version with its stars and stripes looked too much like the Union flag.

A Union envelope featuring Union and rebel flags in 1861

In July 1861, Mary Chesnut wrote of the mood in Confederate Richmond after the last of the eleventh stars joined.

*"Mrs. Wigfall busy as a bee, making a flag for her Texians.... Everybody said at first: 'Pshaw! There will be no war.' Those who foresaw evil were called 'Ravens'—ill foreboders. Now the same sanguine people all cry 'the war is over.'"*

## Cutting

Refer to the blocks for your shading preferences. Decide whether you want an 8″ × 8″ block or a 12″ × 12″ block (12″ × 12″ block measurements are in parentheses). Cut the following:

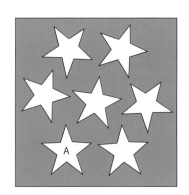

1 background square 8½″ × 8½″ (12½″ × 12½″).

**A:** 7 piece A stars using the pattern (page 110).*

*Remember to add a seam allowance around each appliqué piece if using a turn-under method of appliqué.*

## Reference

*C. Vann Woodward (editor), Mary Chesnut's Civil War (New Haven: Yale University Press, 1993), p. 110.*

## Block 41

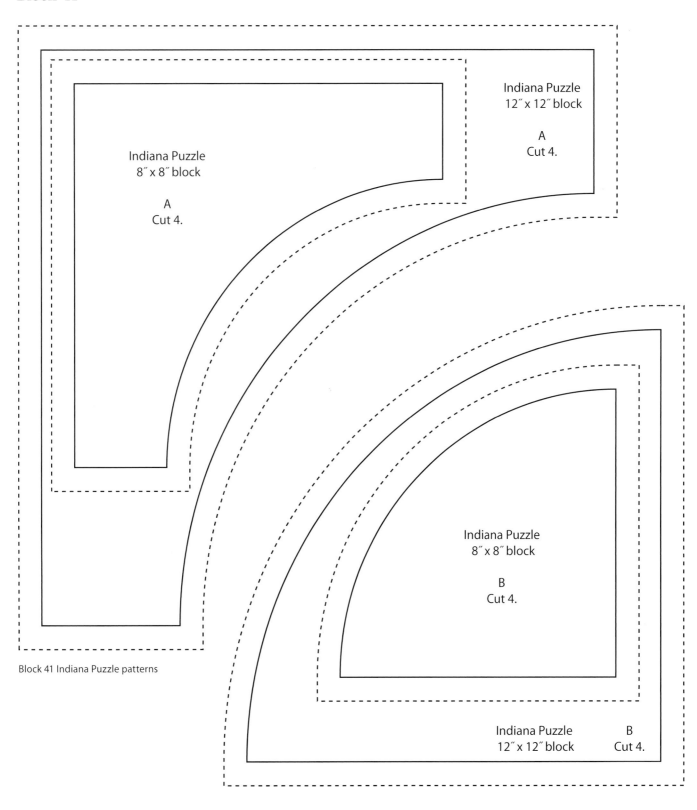

Indiana Puzzle
12″ x 12″ block

A
Cut 4.

Indiana Puzzle
8″ x 8″ block

A
Cut 4.

Indiana Puzzle
8″ x 8″ block

B
Cut 4.

Indiana Puzzle
12″ x 12″ block

B
Cut 4.

Block 41 Indiana Puzzle patterns

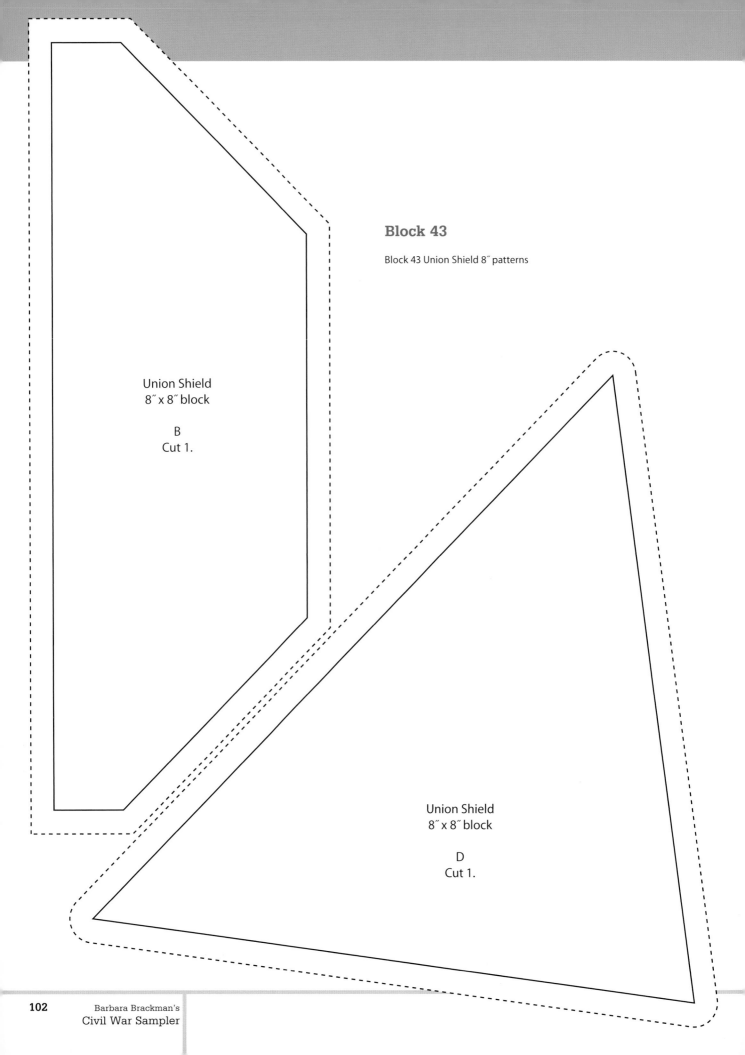

**Block 43**

Block 43 Union Shield 8″ patterns

Union Shield
8″ x 8″ block

B
Cut 1.

Union Shield
8″ x 8″ block

D
Cut 1.

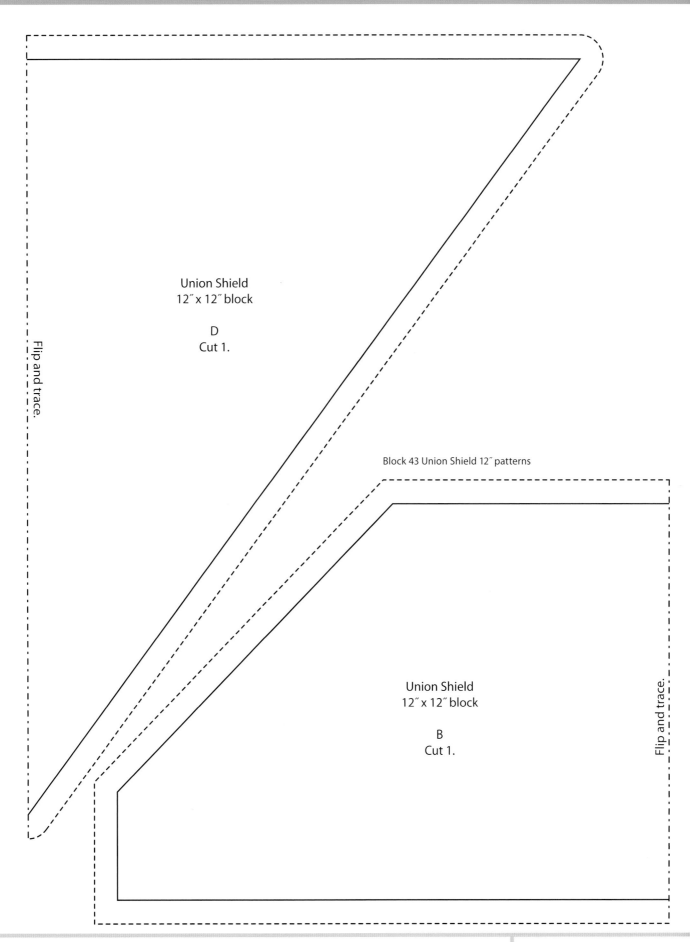

Union Shield
12″ x 12″ block

D
Cut 1.

Flip and trace.

Block 43 Union Shield 12″ patterns

Union Shield
12″ x 12″ block

B
Cut 1.

Flip and trace.

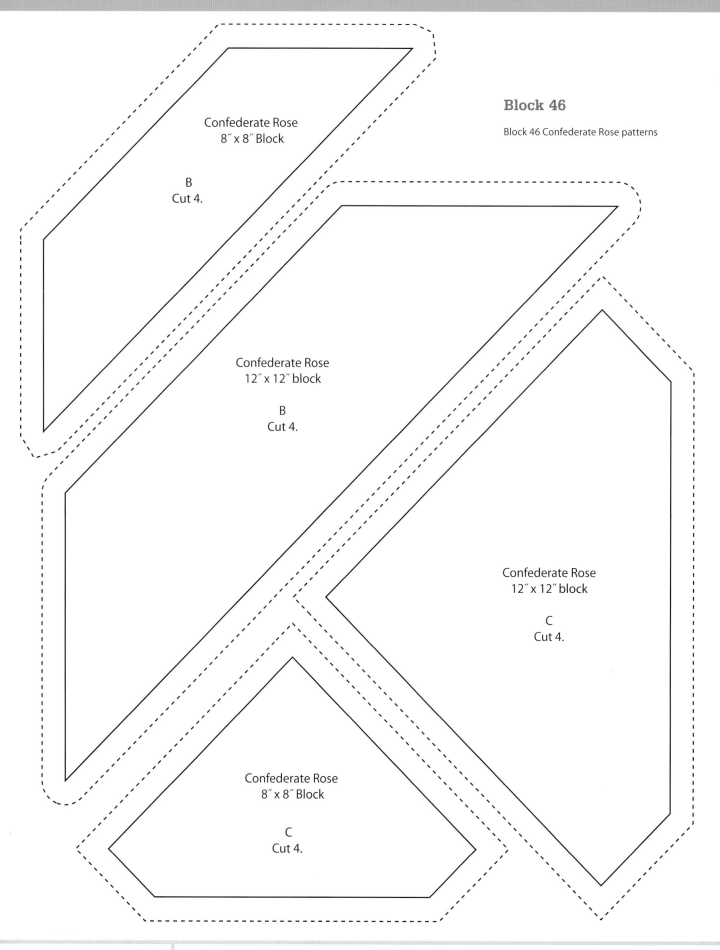

Block 46

Block 46 Confederate Rose patterns

Confederate Rose
8″ x 8″ Block

B
Cut 4.

Confederate Rose
12″ x 12″ block

B
Cut 4.

Confederate Rose
12″ x 12″ block

C
Cut 4.

Confederate Rose
8″ x 8″ Block

C
Cut 4.

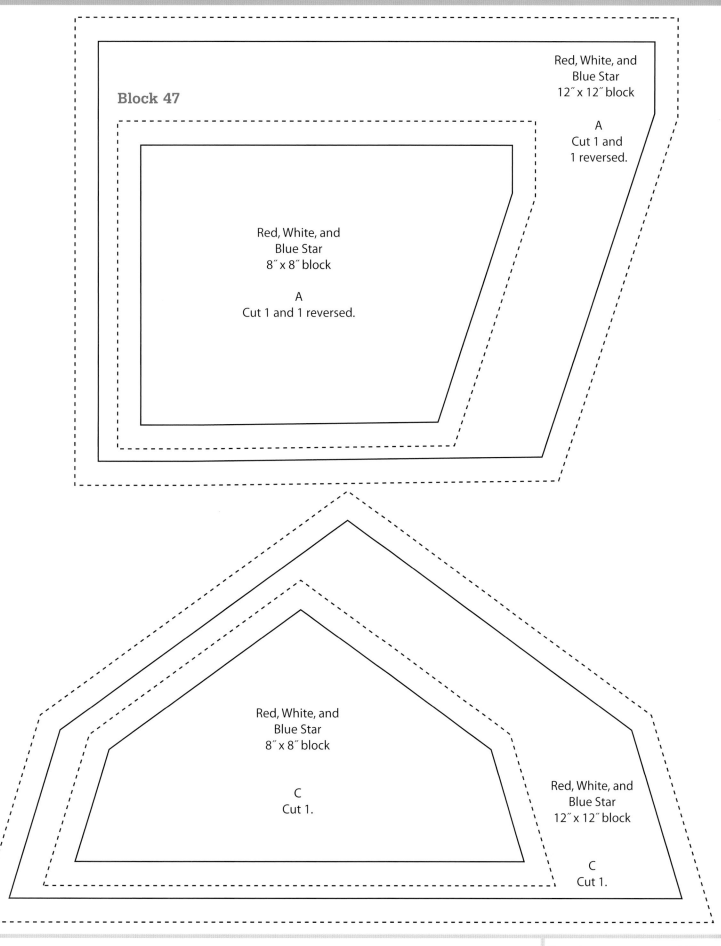

Block 47

Red, White, and
Blue Star
12″ x 12″ block

A
Cut 1 and
1 reversed.

Red, White, and
Blue Star
8″ x 8″ block

A
Cut 1 and 1 reversed.

Red, White, and
Blue Star
8″ x 8″ block

C
Cut 1.

Red, White, and
Blue Star
12″ x 12″ block

C
Cut 1.

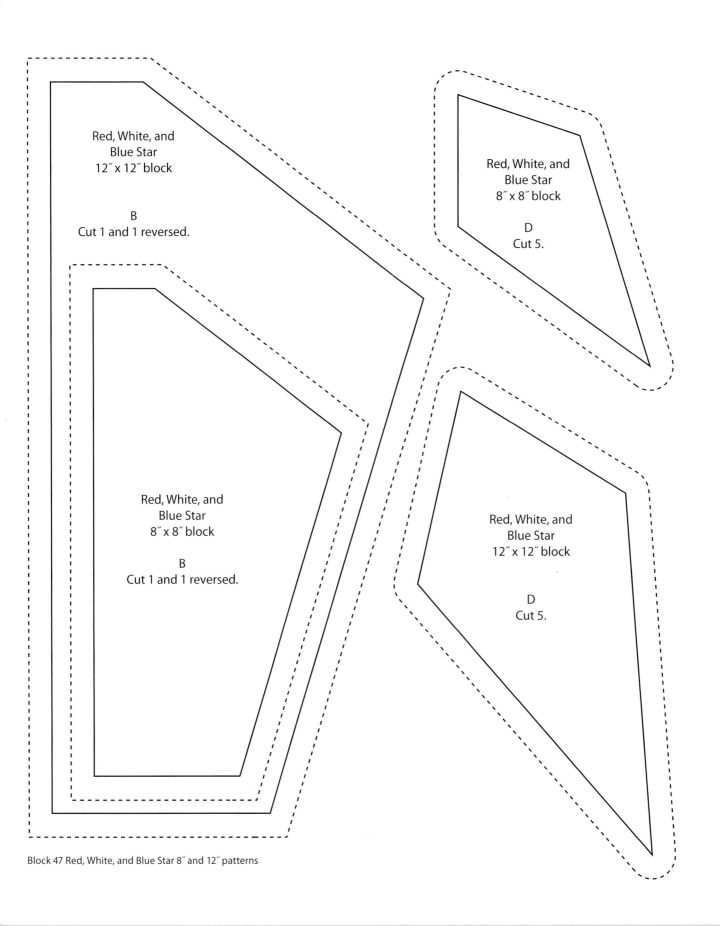

Red, White, and
Blue Star
12″ x 12″ block

B
Cut 1 and 1 reversed.

Red, White, and
Blue Star
8″ x 8″ block

D
Cut 5.

Red, White, and
Blue Star
8″ x 8″ block

B
Cut 1 and 1 reversed.

Red, White, and
Blue Star
12″ x 12″ block

D
Cut 5.

Block 47 Red, White, and Blue Star 8″ and 12″ patterns

## Block 48

Block 48 Stars & Stripes patterns

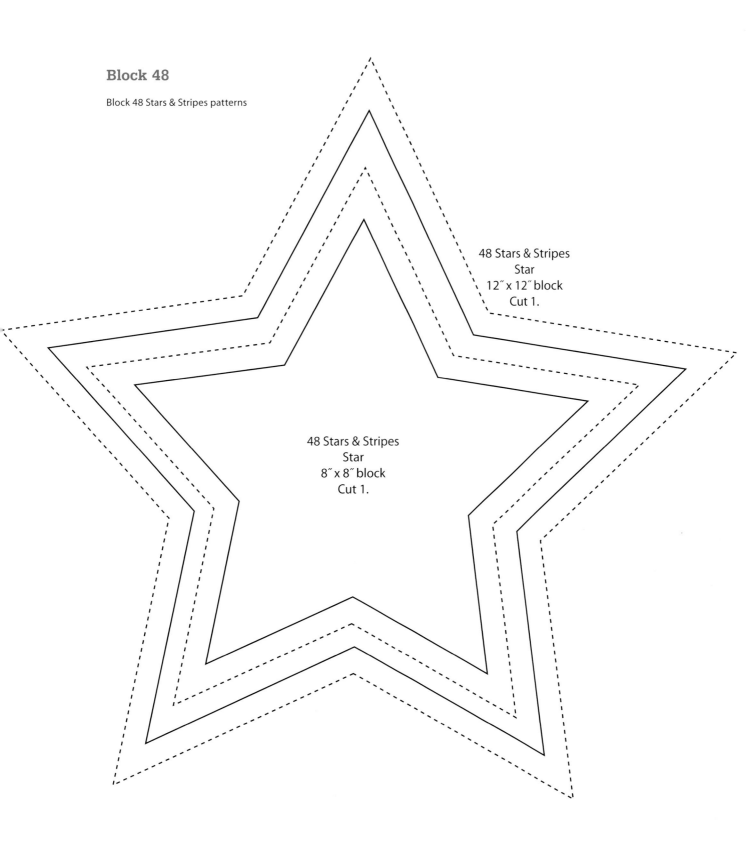

48 Stars & Stripes
Star
12″ x 12″ block
Cut 1.

48 Stars & Stripes
Star
8″ x 8″ block
Cut 1.

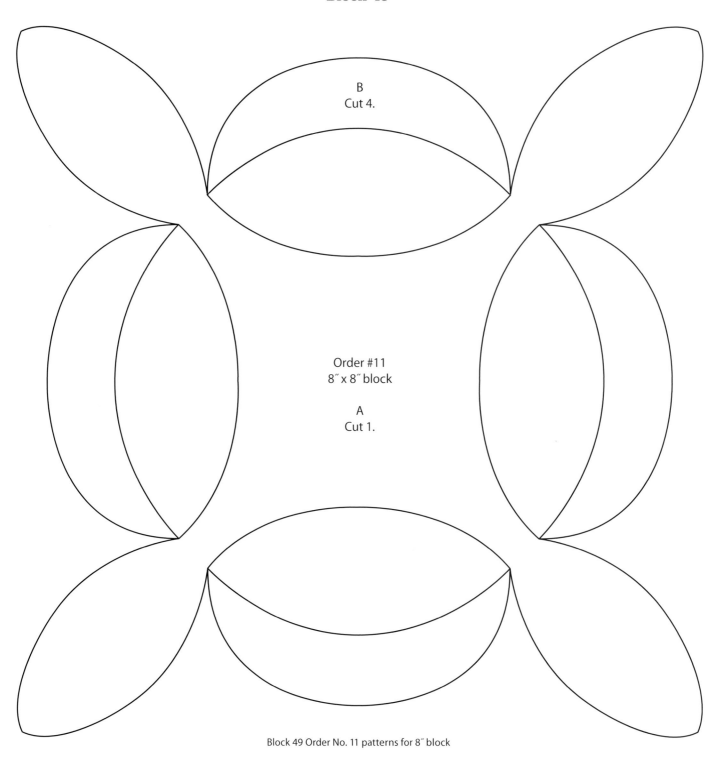

B
Cut 4.

Order #11
8″ x 8″ block

A
Cut 1.

Block 49 Order No. 11 patterns for 8″ block

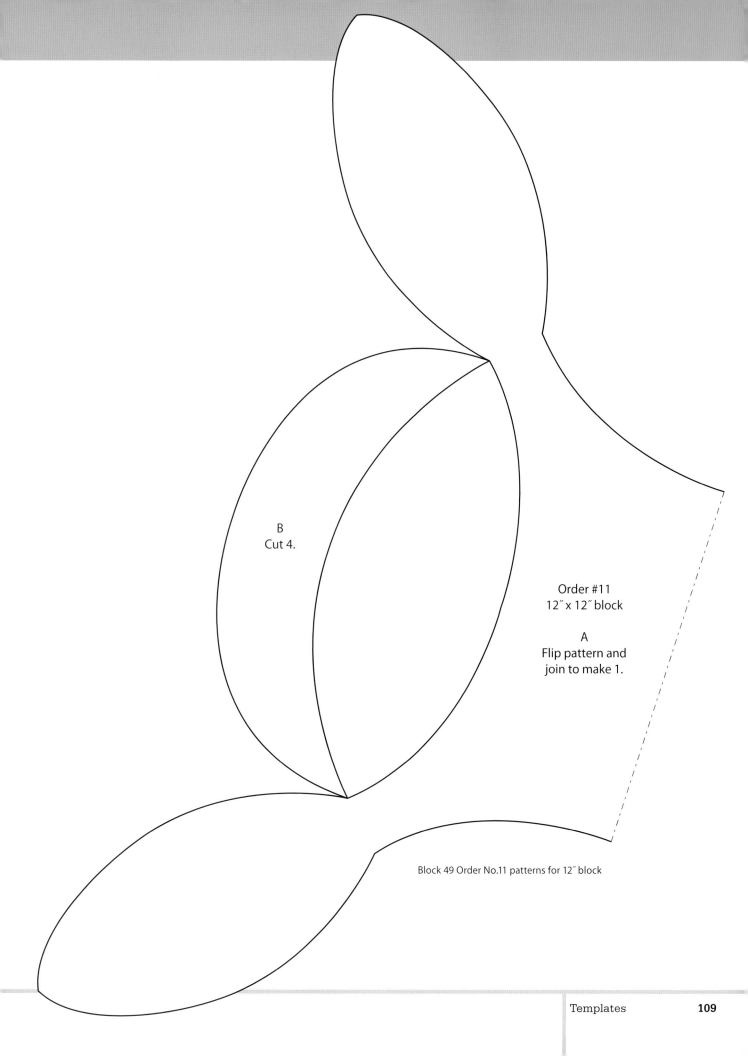

B
Cut 4.

Order #11
12″ x 12″ block

A
Flip pattern and
join to make 1.

Block 49 Order No.11 patterns for 12″ block

**Block 50**

Seven Sisters
8″ x 8″ block
Star
Cut 7.

Seven Sisters
12″ x 12″ block
Star
Cut 7.

Block 50 Seven Sisters patterns

## Also by Barbara Brackman:

 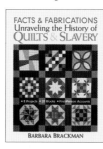   

Available as an eBook only.

Barbara Brackman lives in Lawrence, Kansas, a town with an important Civil War history. She has written several books about quilts and the war, telling the personal stories of women and their handwork. She was a founding member of the American Quilt Study Group and is an honoree of the Quilters Hall of Fame.

# Index

# Great Titles *from* C&T PUBLISHING

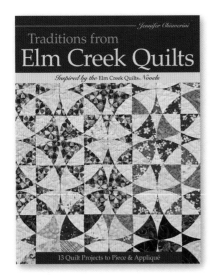

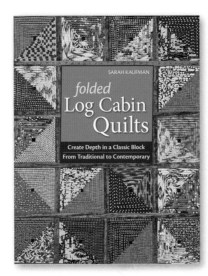

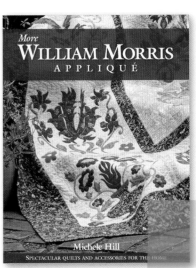

*Available at your local retailer or* **www.ctpub.com** *or* **800-284-1114**

For a list of other fine books from C&T Publishing, visit our website
to view our catalog online.

**C&T PUBLISHING, INC.**
P.O. Box 1456
Lafayette, CA 94549
800-284-1114

Email: ctinfo@ctpub.com
Website: www.ctpub.com

C&T Publishing's professional photography services are now available to
the public. Visit us at www.ctmediaservices.com.

**Tips and Techniques** can be found at www.ctpub.com > Consumer
Resources > Quiltmaking Basics: Tips & Techniques for Quiltmaking & More

For quilting supplies:

**COTTON PATCH**
1025 Brown Ave.
Lafayette, CA 94549
Store: 925-284-1177
Mail order: 925-283-7883

Email: CottonPa@aol.com
Website: www.quiltusa.com

Note: Fabrics shown may not be currently available, as fabric
manufacturers keep most fabrics in print for only a short time.